SPANISH SYNTAX AND COMPOSITION

T0382293

SPANISH SYNTAX
AND
COMPOSITION

by

J. P. HOWARD, M.A.
MILL HILL

CAMBRIDGE
AT THE UNIVERSITY PRESS
1927

CAMBRIDGE
UNIVERSITY PRESS

University Printing House, Cambridge CB2 8BS, United Kingdom

Published in the United States of America by Cambridge University Press, New York

Cambridge University Press is part of the University of Cambridge.

It furthers the University's mission by disseminating knowledge in the pursuit of
education, learning and research at the highest international levels of excellence.

www.cambridge.org
Information on this title: www.cambridge.org/9781107693968

© Cambridge University Press 1927

This publication is in copyright. Subject to statutory exception
and to the provisions of relevant collective licensing agreements,
no reproduction of any part may take place without the written
permission of Cambridge University Press.

First published 1927
First paperback edition 2014

A catalogue record for this publication is available from the British Library

ISBN 978-1-107-69396-8 Paperback

Cambridge University Press has no responsibility for the persistence or accuracy of
URLs for external or third-party internet websites referred to in this publication,
and does not guarantee that any content on such websites is, or will remain, accurate
or appropriate.

PREFACE

This book is intended not for beginners in Spanish but for those who have worked through the Accidence together with some elementary reading and composition. On the other hand the book does not claim to present an exhaustive treatment of Spanish Syntax, but rather to furnish the necessary and sufficient material for more advanced composition.

The Sentences at the end of the book are miscellaneous and colloquial in type. Those at the end of each chapter illustrate the rules of the chapter in question and contain some revision of the chapters preceding. The Prose Selections are translations from Spanish, especially chosen for their idiomatic character. It is assumed that at this stage a dictionary is in use.

All the Spanish Examples have been revised by Señor Luis Delgado of London, and my sincere thanks are due to Mr J. E. Whitehead for his painstaking revision of the proofs.

J. P. HOWARD

MILL HILL
January 1927

CONTENTS

CHAPTER I

THE ARTICLES

(a) DEFINITE

§ 1. The Definite Article is used with:

1. Nouns taken in a general sense.
2. Nouns taken in a particular sense including other parts of speech used as nouns.
3. The verb 'tener' in reference to body and mind.
4. Titles and sometimes ordinary proper names.
5. Measure and weight.
6. Geographical names unless, with few exceptions, governed by a preposition.
7. The infinitive to form a noun.
8. A proper noun preceded by an adjective and *de*.
9. (In the neuter) adjectives to form a noun or exclamatory phrase.

The Definite Article is omitted with:

10. Succession of kings, etc.
11. Repetition of a comparative.
12. Names of languages, except *el castellano*, when placed *immediately* after the verb *hablar*.

§ 2. *Examples.*

1. Los hombres aman la virtud.	Men love virtue.
2. (*a*) El francés y el alemán son las lenguas que aprendo.	French and German are the languages I am learning.
(*b*) El sí y el no.	The 'yes' and 'no.'
3. Ella tiene los ojos azules.	She has blue eyes.
4. (*a*) El rey don Alfonso con el general Rivera.	King Alphonso with General Rivera.
(*b*) El viejo Pedro.	Old Peter.
5. Dos pesetas la libra.	Two pesetas a pound.

6. (a) La España y la Gran Bretaña. — Spain and Great Britain.

(b) Yo voy de Francia a Bélgica. — I am going from France to Belgium.

7. El hablar puede ser útil. — Speaking may be useful.

8. El pobre (de) Juan. — Poor John.

9. (a) ¡Lo claro de la frase! — How clear the sentence is!

(b) ¡Lo hermosas que son! — How beautiful they are!

(c) Lo bueno es agradable. — The (what is) good is pleasing.

10. Carlos Quinto padre de Felipe Segundo. — Charles the Fifth father of Philip the Second.

11. Cuanto más yo leo (tanto) más yo aprendo. — The more I read the more I learn.

12. Él no puede hablar alemán, pero habla bien el francés. — He cannot speak German, but he speaks French well.

(b) INDEFINITE

§ 3. The Indefinite Article is used with:

1. Nouns of an indeterminate character.

The Indefinite Article is omitted with:

2. A noun in apposition.
3. A noun used as predicate to the verb 'to be.'
4. *Qué* in exclamations.
5. A negative or plural.
6. *Otro. Cierto. Ciento. Mil.*

§ 4. *Examples.*

1. Un caballo. Un número. Una comida. — A horse. A number. A meal.

2. Velázquez, pintor español. — Velazquez, a Spanish painter.

3. Él es limpiabotas. — He is a boot-cleaner.

4. ¡Qué (cuál) bonita mantilla! — What a pretty shawl!

5. (a) Yo no tengo cuchillo. — I haven't a knife.

(b) ¿Hay aceitunas en la mesa? — Are there any olives on the table?

6. Otro hombre apareció. — Another man appeared.

(c) PARTITIVE

§ 5. The Partitive Article can always be omitted.

§ 6. *Examples.*

(a) Yo compraré pan.	I will buy bread.
(b) Nosotros no tenemos vino.	We haven't any wine.
(c) ¿Desea Vd. libros ingleses?	Do you want (some) English books?
(d) Había ovejas y corderos en el campo.	Some sheep and lambs were in the field.

I. *Translate:*

1. Students take lessons with masters every morning.
2. Here are the pens and the blotting paper.
3. Donkeys have long ears.
4. King George and Queen Mary were present with Queen Victoria of Spain.
5. Switzerland is a mountainous country.
6. He passed through Germany on his way to Russia.
7. Reading in bed is harmful to the eyes.
8. Avoid always all that is ugly.
9. He was one of Louis XIV's gardeners.
10. The less he looks for the less he finds.
11. My son speaks Spanish fairly well; he is now learning English.
12. This cloth is worth ten shillings a yard.
13. My brother was a good friend in bad times.
14. Have you the works of Baroja, a Spanish novelist?
15. My father is a sculptor, the best sculptor in the world.
16. What a fine bridge there is at Córdova!
17. Haven't you a key? Then we can't get in.
18. I can't buy that house; there is no bathroom in it.
19. Put another fireplace in the dining-room, instead of that ugly one.
20. We saw some ink and some inkwells in the shop.

CHAPTER II

THE NOUN

§ 7. 1. Two nouns may be coupled together in complementary treatment.

2. Some nouns of kinship or rank in the masculine plural may be masculine and feminine in meaning.

3. Feminine nouns beginning with accented *a* or *ha* are preceded by the masculine form of the Definite Article in the singular[1].

§ 8. *Examples.*

1. (*a*) Una botella para vino.　　A wine-bottle.
   (*b*) Un tiro de fusil.　　　　　A gun-shot.
   (*c*) Una tarde de verano.　　　A summer evening.
2. (*a*) Los hijos de los reyes.　　The children (sons and daughters) of the king and queen.
   (*b*) Mis padres y mis abuelos.　My parents and grandparents.
   (*c*) Una invitación de mis tíos.　An invitation from my uncle and aunt.
3. El ala del águila.　　　　　　The eagle's wing.

II. *Translate :*

1. There are tea-cups and spoons in the cupboard.
2. Children like to play with tin soldiers.
3. We shall have mutton cutlets this even.ng.
4. One cold winter morning the water froze in our house.
5. I will bring with me John and Mary, my nephew and niece.
6. My brother and sisters are at school now.

1 In such cases *del* and *al* must be used for *de la* and *a la* respectively : e.g. *del hacha, al agua.*

CHAPTER III

THE ADJECTIVE

(a) QUALIFYING

§ 9. The Qualifying Adjective:

1. Agrees with the noun it qualifies.
2. Takes the masculine form with nouns of two genders.
3. Is generally placed after the noun qualified; is always so placed when expressing colour, shape, nationality, religion; or in the case of a past participle used as an adjective. A few common adjectives nearly always precede the noun.
4. Used in (a) a figurative sense or (b) expressing the essential quality of the noun may precede the noun.
5. *Grande* changes its meaning according to its position.
6. *Bueno, malo*[1] omit the final *o* before masculine nouns in the singular, and *grande* the final *de* before masculine and feminine nouns in the singular.

§ 10. *Examples.*

1. El hijo orgulloso de una familia castellana.
   The proud son of a Castilian family.
2. Son antiguos la catedral y el alcázar.
   The cathedral and the alcázar are old.
3. (a) Resultó un desastre terrible.
   There was a terrible disaster.
   (b) El me entregó su pañuelo rojo.
   He handed me his red handkerchief.
   (c) Se halló en un cuarto redondo.
   He was in a round room.
   (d) Un obispo de la iglesia anglicana.
   A bishop of the Anglican Church.
   (e) Yo tropecé con un hombre desconocido.
   I ran into a stranger.
   (f) 'Buena suerte,' ellos nos gritaron.
   'Good luck' they cried to us.

1 Also *primero, tercero, uno, alguno, ninguno. Santo* drops final *to* before masculine nouns except *Domingo* and *Tomás*: e.g. *San Felipe* but *Santo Domingo, Santo Tomás.*

(g) Ellos vivieron en malos tiempos.	They lived in bad times.
(h) El viejo perro era ciego.	The old dog was blind.
(i) Una linda niña me dió un clavel.	A pretty little girl gave me a carnation.
(j) ¿Dónde están las mejores escuelas?	Where are the best schools?
4. (a) Una estrecha amistad.	A close friendship.
(b) La blanquísima nieve de la sierra.	The (very) white snow of the mountain range.
5. (a) Sevilla tiene una gran catedral.	Seville has a fine cathedral.
(b) Goliat fué un hombre grande[1].	Goliath was a huge man.
6. (a) Hay muy buen azúcar aquí.	There is much good sugar here.
(b) No me traiga Vd. mal vino.	Don't bring me bad wine.
(c) San Pablo y San Lucas fueron escritores célebres.	St Paul and St Luke were famous writers.
(d) La gran reina de este gran pueblo.	The great queen of this great people.

III. *Translate:*

1. The yellow and blue flowers are planted together.
2. His lip and cheek were covered with blood.
3. Prisoners are unhappy people in their solitary lives.
4. Will you show me some brown shoes?
5. The town hall is a large square building.
6. In Spanish history much is said of the devotion to the Catholic Faith.
7. English books usually have cut pages.
8. A very large black cat sprang from the table to the floor.
9. The rain came through this bad roof.
10. In the middle of the town was a little square.
11. The citizens enjoyed wide liberty.
12. There aren't many green fields in Castile.

1 Cf. also: cierta noticia, certain news; noticia cierta, true news.
        mala lengua, slanderer; lengua mala, sore tongue.
        pobre hombre, poor man; hombre pobre, a poor man.

(b) Numeral

§ 11. 1. The cardinal numeral is used to express *dates* except the first of the month, and *de* must be placed between the date and the month and between the month and the year.

2. *Age* may be expressed by *tener* followed by the number of years.

3. To express *time* the definite article precedes the hour; the word *hora(s)* is omitted; the hours precede parts of the hour which are either added or deducted, and the conjunction *y* must precede the part added to the hour. Finally the singular of the verb is used with *one o'clock*, *midday* and *midnight* only.

4. Cardinal numbers are invariable except *uno* and compounds of *ciento*. *Ciento* takes the sign of the plural and agrees in gender only when multiplied by a number, and is written *cien* before a noun and *mil* when not multiplied by a number.

5. *Dimension* is expressed by the verbs *ser* or *tener* followed by one of four alternative forms of expression.

6. The ordinal numeral is used after names of sovereigns (etc.) up to *ten*; subsequently the cardinal.

7. The ordinal numbers *primero* and *tercero* lose their final *o* before a masculine singular noun. (cf. § 9. 6.)

8. Counting in hundreds is not employed after *nine hundred*.

§ 12. *Examples.*

1. El primero (1) y el tres (3) de Junio de 1920.

The first (1st) and third (3rd) of June 1920.

2. Yo tendré diez (10) años el mes próximo.

I shall be ten (10) next month.

3. (*a*) Es la una; dentro de una hora serán las dos.

It is one o'clock; in an hour it will be two.

(*b*) Venga Vd. a las cinco y media o a las seis menos diez.

Come at half-past five or at ten minutes to six.

4. (*a*) Ella ha comprado las tres casas.   She has bought the three houses.

  (*b*) Cincuenta y una mujeres.   Fifty-one women.

  (*c*) Las manzanas valen cien pesetas.   The apples are worth a hundred pesetas.

5. (*a*) Este cuarto tiene (es de) 50 pies de ancho.   This room is 50 feet wide.

  (*b*) Este cuarto tiene (es de) 50 pies de anchura.   ,, ,, ,,

  (*c*) Este cuarto tiene una anchura de 50 pies.   ,, ,, ,,

6. Luis Catorce se hizo amigo con el rey de Inglaterra.   Louis the Fourteenth became a friend of the king of England.

7. El primer hotel que yo ví.   The first hotel I saw.

8. Yo gané mil quinientas pesetas.   I earned fifteen hundred pesetas.

IV. *Translate:*

1. The dance will take place on the 25th of June.
2. My grandson was five years old last year.
3. The doors will be shut after half-past five.
4. Why doesn't the bell ring? It is twelve o'clock.
5. In his farm there are five hundred sheep.
6. This magnificent cathedral is 200 feet long.
7. I will tell you something about Charles the Fifth.
8. You are the third boy who has forgotten his book.
9. In the year 1789 the French Revolution broke out.
10. A thousand years seem a long time.

(*c*) POSSESSIVE

§ 13. The Possessive Adjective:

1. Agrees with the object possessed.
2. May be replaced by the definite article when the reference is to something inseparable from the person.
3. Is often added to the noun in familiar or polite style.
4. To avoid ambiguity may be completed by the disjunctive personal pronoun.

5. In the second person singular indicates familiar or superior relationship, and in the second person plural indicates either familiar relationship to more than one person or formal courtesy to one or more persons. (cf. § 20. 3.)

§ 14. *Examples.*

1. Nuestra madre ha llegado con sus amigos.	Our mother has arrived with her friends.
2. (*a*) Ellos levantaron los ojos al cielo.	They raised their eyes to heaven.
(*b*) Se le ha conservado la vida.	His life has been preserved.
3. (*a*) Yo obedezco, mi general.	I obey, general (sir).
(*b*) No me olvide Vd., madre mía[1].	Do not forget me, mother.
4. Era su hermana (de él) que vino.	It was his sister who came.
5. (*a*) Tus amigos, hermano, son míos.	Your friends, brother, are mine.
(*b*) Toma tu hueso, perro.	Take your bone, dog.
(*c*) Llevad vuestros paraguas, niños.	Take your umbrellas with you, children.
(*d*) Yo pido vuestro amparo, señores.	I ask for your support, gentlemen.

V. *Translate:*

1. We have sold our country house for twelve hundred pounds.
2. Wash your faces and hands before one o'clock.
3. I have cut my finger. What bad luck!
4. Here is some good wine, colonel. Taste it.
5. It is their house, not yours, that is burning.
6. Dear mother, I shall write to you on the first of each month.
7. You ought to wear your warm clothes, little girls.
8. You will vote, gentlemen, according to your consciences.

1 The forms *mio*, *tuyo* etc. should be used with caution.

(d) Miscellaneous

Below are given a number of examples showing the use of the common miscellaneous or indefinite adjectives.

§ 15. *Examples.*

1. Todo.

(a) Yo trabajaba todo el día.	I was working all day.
(b) Todo hombre necesita dormir.	Every man needs sleep.
(c) Los soldados vinieron de todas partes.	The soldiers came in from every direction.
(d) Lo he visto todo.	I have seen everything.
(e) Todo lo que pasaba me inspiraba dolor.	All that was happening caused me sorrow.
(f) Iremos todos al teatro.	All of us will go to the theatre.
(g) Toda una casa se quemó.	One entire house was burnt.

2. Cada.

Había veinte personas, y cada paisano llevaba una manta.	There were twenty persons, and each peasant was wearing a cloak.

3. Solo.

Ni una sola persona me escuchó.	Not a single person listened to me.

4. Alguno.

(a) Algunas hojas cayeron del árbol.	Some leaves fell from the tree.
(b) No había habitaciones algunas[1].	There weren't any rooms.

5. Ninguno.

(a) Ningún pueblo tenía agua.	No city had water.
(b) No tenía agua ningún pueblo[2].	,, ,, ,, ,,

6. Mismo.

(a) Ella se sentó a la misma mesa.	She sat at the same table.

1 I.e. *negative* in meaning when placed *after* the noun qualified.

2 *Ninguno* and *alguno* lose the final 'o' before a masculine noun or adjective. (cf. § 11, 7.)

(*b*) Aquí, en este sitio mismo, Nelson murió.

Here, on this very spot, Nelson died.

(*c*) Ellos mismos salieron.

They themselves went out.

7. Cualquiera.

    (*a*) Busque Vd. a un hombre cualquiera.

Look for some man or other (any man).

    (*b*) Tome Vd. cualesquiera libros que le gusten.

Take whatever books you like.

8. Tal.

    (*a*) Tal causa debe producir tal efecto.

Such a cause ought to (must) produce such an effect.

    (*b*) Yo no tengo telo tal como Vd. desea.

I haven't such cloth as you want.

    (*c*) Un tal Fernando vino a verme.

A certain Ferdinand came to see me.

9. Otro. (cf. § 3. 6.)

Mozo, traiga otro plato.

Waiter, bring another plate.

10. Cierto. (cf. § 3. 6.)

Visité cierto restaurant con ellos.

I visited a certain restaurant with them.

11. Propio.

    (*a*) Él lo vió con sus propios ojos.

He saw it with his own eyes.

    (*b*) Es una medicina muy propia para él.

It is a very suitable medicine for him.

12. Mucho.

    (*a*) Los obreros tenían mucha hambre.

The workmen were very hungry.

    (*b*) Mucho pan fué vendido por el panadero.

A lot of bread was sold by the baker.

13. Poco.

    (*a*) Pocos caminos había allí derechos.

Few roads there were straight.

    (*b*) Un poco de[1] azúcar, hágame el favor.

A little sugar, please.

14. Demasiado.

Hay demasiada leche en esta taza.

There is too much milk in this cup.

---

1 *Un poco de* may be regarded as an adjectival expression.

15. Bastante.

Mande Vd. frutas bastantes[1] para todo el mundo.

Send enough fruit for everyone.

16. Alguno que otro.

Algunas que otras señoras paseaban en el jardín.

A few ladies were walking in the garden.

17. Unos cuantos.

Unos cuantos mendigos estaban sentados en la puerta.

A few beggars were sitting in the doorway.

18. Ambos. Uno y otro.

A la una ambas (una y otra) tienda(s) estaban cerradas.

At one o'clock both shops were shut.

19. El demás.

(a) Yo quedé en casa, los demás se fueron.

I remained in the house (at home), the rest went.

(b) Después de la comida yo le diré lo demás.

After dinner I will tell you the rest.

20. Ajeno.

No se entremeta Vd. con los asuntos ajenos.

Don't interfere with other people's affairs.

21. Sendos.

Seis señores con sendos caballos se acercaron.

Six gentlemen approached, having one horse each.

VI. *Translate:*

1. The dazzling white snow lay on the ground the whole week.
2. You need not speak; he has confessed everything.
3. All that he forgot I remember.
4. Each gipsy-girl danced once.
5. The Church should be one single body, united and indivisible.
6. Some Spanish soldiers examined our luggage at the frontier.
7. There are no candles upstairs.
8. The theatre and the university are in the same street.
9. I myself have travelled as much as you.
10. Any of the questions may be answered in any order.
11. Why has such a town such an ugly bridge?
12. Another cup, Mary, please!
13. On a certain spring evening at a quarter to seven, I met him for the first time.

1 Or *bastante de.*

14. This is a helmet of my own invention, said the White Knight.
15. The architect was very ashamed when he saw his work completed.
16. Few painters become rich.
17. Too many mice live in this old house, and not enough cats.
18. He lent both the walking sticks and kept the umbrella.
19. After drinking some water, he ate the rest of the food.
20. What belongs to others does not interest me.

(e) COMPARISON OF ADJECTIVES

(N.B. Adverbial expressions of Comparison are most conveniently treated here.)

§ 16. The following are the customary expressions of comparison:

1. *Tan*, as ...*como*, as; *más*, more ...*que*, than; *menos*, less ...*que*, than.
2. *Tanto*, as (so) much (many) ...*como*, as; *tan*, so ...*que*, that.
   Tanto, so much (many) ...*que*, that.
3. *Cuanto más* (*menos*), the more (less) ...*tanto más* (*menos*), the more (less).
   Cada vez más (*menos*), more (less) and more (less).
4. *Tanto más cuanto*, so much (all) the more as.
5. 'Than' when followed by a number is translated by *de*[1].
6. 'Than' introducing a clause including a verb is translated by *de lo que*, *del que*, *de los que*, etc.
7. Adjectives made superlative by inflection can only be used in *absolute* not *relative* sense.

§ 17. *Examples.*

1. (a) Yo soy tan alto como él.   I am as tall as he.
   (b) Él es más grande que su padre.   He is bigger than his father.
   (c) Esta calle es menos concurrida que aquella.   This street is less crowded than that.

---

1 Except in the expression *no...más que* which never changes even when followed by a number: e.g. *No tengo más que diez libros.*

2. (a) Él mostró tanta fortaleza como (que) yo. — He showed as much fortitude as I.

(b) Vd. gasta tanto como ellos. — You spend as much as they.

(c) Estaba tan lluvioso que no era posible salir. — It was so rainy that it was not possible to go out.

(d) Había tanta gente que no pude entrar. — There were so many people that I couldn't go in.

3. (a) Cuanto más nieva (tanto) más difícil es andar. — The more it snows the more difficult it is to walk.

(b) Cuanto menos yo como (tanto) más hambre tengo. — The less I eat the hungrier I am.

(c) Ella se puso cada vez más pálida. — She became paler and paler (more and more pale).

4. Yo saldré ahora tanto más cuanto no llueve. — I shall go out now, all the more as it is not raining.

5. Fueron muertos más de doce toros. — More than twelve bulls were killed.

6. Vd. duerme más de lo que es necesario. — You sleep more than is necessary.

7. (a) Un hermosísimo paisaje de Suiza. — A most beautiful landscape in Switzerland.

(b) El chico más feo de la aldea. — The ugliest little boy in the village.

VII. *Translate:*

1. Happiness comes as often as misfortune.
2. Falsehood is less honourable than truth.
3. Life is more inspiring than death.
4. You are not as cowardly as I am.
5. He was so uncertain that I could not trust him.
6. The less you offend the more you will please us.
7. The steamer went faster and faster.
8. I shall sell it now, all the more as its value is greater than it was.
9. I have seen more than ten new roads near London.
10. He knew more than he pretended to know.
11. There is a very dangerous turning between here and the station.
12. The greater part of the travellers stayed where they were.

CHAPTER IV

THE PRONOUN

(a) PERSONAL CONJUNCTIVE

§ **18.** As subject:

1. The pronoun may be omitted in verb conjugation; but in the case of *Vd.*, *Vds.*, these should be employed on their first occurrence to avoid ambiguity.

2. The reflexive pronoun *se* is also used to translate *one*, *you*, *they*, etc.[1]

3. *Vd.* (*vuestra merced*), *Vds.* (*vuestras mercedes*) correspond to the English *you* in ordinary conversation; they require the third person of the verb. *Vosotros*, besides being the plural of *tu* and used for addressing more than one person in familiar relationship, is also used of *one* person to mark extreme courtesy or formality. It is also used in public notices, parliamentary speeches, addresses, etc. (cf. § 13. 5.)

As object:

4. Direct or indirect, the pronoun usually precedes the verb. With the Infinitive, Present Participle and Affirmative Commands, however, the pronoun follows the verb and forms one word with it. When two pronouns occur in conjunction the indirect always precedes the direct, and in the case of two pronouns of the third person, the indirect, for the sake of euphony, is always *se*.

5. The pronouns *la*, *lo*, *los*, *las* are used as complements of the verbs *ser*, *estar* and *tener*.

6. The pronoun is often employed as object in a redundant sense.

---

1 In this sense *se* may often be treated as a reflexive.

§ 19. *Examples.*

1. (*a*) Saqué mi dinero que me llevaron.

   I took out my money which they took from me.

   (*b*) Vd. sabe lo que quiero decir y debe entenderlo.

   You know what I mean and you ought to understand.

2. (*a*) Se dice que el ministro ha muerto.

   It is said that the minister has died.

   (*b*) Aquí se habla Italiano.

   Italian is spoken here.

3. (*a*) ¿Quieren Vds. accompañarme?

   Will you accompany me?

   (*b*) Tenéis mucho frío, hijos míos.

   You are very cold, children.

   (*c*) Podéis entrar en esta casa como en la vuestra.

   You may come into this house as into your own.

   (*d*) Empujad (vosotros) la puerta.

   Push the door.

   (*e*) Debéis apoyar al rey, señores.

   You should support the king, gentlemen.

4. (*a*) Lo perderé pronto.

   I shall lose it soon.

   (*b*) No me diga Vd. eso.

   Don't tell me that.

   (*c*) Me los han enseñado.

   They have shown them to me.

   (*d*) El cochero se lo dió (a Vd.).

   The coachman gave it to you.

   (*e*) Quiere mostrárnoslos.

   He wants to show them to us.

   (*f*) Levantándome de la cama, caí.

   Getting out of bed, I fell.

   (*g*) Búsquelo Vd. en seguida.

   Find it at once.

5. (*a*) ¿Es Vd. soldado? Lo soy.

   Are you a soldier? I am.

   (*b*) La tierra estaba mojada, no lo está ahora.

   The ground was wet; now it is not.

   (*c*) ¿Tiene Vd. plumas? No las tengo.

   Have you pens? I have not.

6. El hijo le vió a su padre.

   The son saw his father.

VIII. *Translate:*

1. I promised to do it when he came.
2. Obey the officers always and answer their questions sensibly.
3. The story is told how the brave hero defended the bridge.
4. Smoking is permitted in most theatres but not in this.
5. You deserve better luck than you have had, my friends.

6. May I offer you a seat, sir?
7. Brush your hair, and hurry up. I will wait for you.
8. I forced myself to eat some breakfast.
9. She knows him because my father-in-law introduced him to her.
10. Pronounce it slowly and carefully.
11. I will give you the exercises. Bring them on Thursday and don't forget them.
12. I will come and show them to him.
13. Meat here used to be tender; now it isn't.
14. These silver forks aren't cheap. I think they are.
15. The more they forgave their brother the less he improved.

(b) Personal Disjunctive

§ 20. The Disjunctive Pronoun is used:

1. After a preposition.
2. After verbs of motion.
3. After a verb and adjective to remove ambiguity or add emphasis.

§ 21. *Examples.*

1. Jugaré contigo y con ella. — I shall play with you and her.
2. Ella corrió hacia mí con una carta. — She ran to me with a letter.
3. (a) Se lo prestó a ella. — He lent it to her.
   (b) ¿Cómo está su padre de Vd.? — How is your father?

IX. *Translate:*

1. He determined to go without her.
2. They came to us asking for bread.
3. He converted *him*, his own father.
4. Clean *his* shoes, not mine.
5. I drove with them to the station road.
6. To-morrow morning go to her and ask her for a dance ticket.

(c) Possessive

§ 22. 1. With the verb *ser* the disjunctive pronoun may take the place of the possessive.

2. For the sake of clearness the possessive pronoun may be replaced by *el* (etc.) *de.*

§ 23. *Examples.*

1. Este sombrero es de él.   This hat is his.
2. No puedo hallar mis guantes   I cannot find my gloves or yours.
   ni los de Vd.

(d) Demonstrative

§ 24. Examples are given below showing the use of the following demonstrative pronouns.

1. Éste; ése, aquél.
   - (a) Mire Vd. los dos caminos;   Look at the two roads; this one
     éste es mejor que aquél.   is better than that.
   - (b) Juan y Pedro vendrán;   John and Peter will come; the
     éste, mañana.   latter, to-morrow.
2. Ello; esto, eso, aquello.
   - (a) Lo olvidó y se fué sin ello.   He forgot it and went away without it.
   - (b) Sin esto no volveré a   Without this I shall not work
     trabajar.   again.
3. El que; el de.
   - (a) Los que hagan eso serán   Those who do that will be
     castigados.   punished.
   - (b) Venderé nuestras peras y   I shall sell our pears and the
     las del vecino.   neighbour's.
4. He aquí.
   He aquí la estación!   This (here) is the station.

N.B. The Demonstrative *Adjective este, aquel* etc. has been omitted, not requiring any special treatment.

X. *Translate:*

1. He gave me a hat which was not mine.
2. Your tooth-brush is with mine in that large drawer.
3. Will you lend me your razor? This one is not sharp.

4. He always plays with people who beat him.
5. Here are towels. Give one to everyone.
6. Your gardener will sell his own fruit with his master's.

(e) RELATIVE

§ 25. 1. The words *que* and *quien* when occurring as objects in a sentence can never be omitted as in English.

2. *El cual, el que* should generally be used when they indicate a *thing* and are immediately preceded by a preposition. They also remove ambiguity because they indicate number and gender.

3. *Lo cual, lo que* is used as a relative when the antecedent is the sense of a clause or complex expression.

4. *Quien* can take the place of *el que* in the nominative case.

5. *Quienes...quienes* can be used to translate *some...others.*

6. *De que* forms an expression giving the equivalent of cause or means.

7. Governing prepositions must precede the relative.

8. *Cuyo* (etc.) can only be used in relative clauses[1].

9. *Que* can be used of persons or things; *quien* only of persons.

10. *All who, all which, all that* may be translated by *cuanto* (etc.).

§ 26. *Examples.*

1. (a) Las flores que cogí están muertas. — The flowers I picked are dead.

  (b) Es el solo (único) abogado a quien conozco. — He is the only lawyer I know.

2. (a) La tiza con la cual (con la que, con que) escribió. — The chalk with which he wrote.

  (b) El pasaporte sin el que (sin el cual, sin que) no puedo pasar la frontera. — The passport without which I cannot cross the frontier.

    1 *Cuyo* may be classed as a possessive Adjective.

(c) Tengo romances y novelas, las cuales no me gustan.

I have ballads and tales, which (i.e. tales) I do not like.

3. Se arrojó de la ventana; lo cual (que) era peligroso.

He threw himself from the window; which was dangerous.

4. (a) Quien canta sus penas espanta.

He who sings frightens away his troubles.

(b) Era de quienes estaban conmigo.

It belonged to those who were with me.

5. Llegaron, quienes a pie, quienes a caballo.

They arrived, some on foot, some on horseback.

(a) Hay de qué burlarse.

There is something to laugh about.

(b) No hay de qué.

It doesn't matter. Not at all.

7. (a) El museo en que (el cual) estamos es célebre.

The museum we are in is celebrated.

(b) ¿Cómo se llama el pueblo a donde vamos?

What is the name of the town we are going to?

8. (a) Éste es el señor en cuya casa (en la casa de quien, del cual, del que) yo quedaba.

This is the gentleman in whose house I stayed.

(b) Visitemos al alcalde cuya cortesía (la cortesía de quien, del cual, del que) aprecio mucho.

Let us visit the mayor whose courtesy I much appreciate.

9. (a) ¿Permítame presentarle a mi hermana de quien hablé ayer?

May I introduce you to my sister of whom I spoke yesterday?

(b) He perdido el lápiz que compré.

I have lost the pencil I bought.

10. Pidió noticias a cuantos vinieron.

He asked all who came for news.

XI. *Translate:*

1. Will you wash the gloves I wore yesterday?
2. Many are the kings that archbishop has crowned.
3. Here is a black veil through which you can see clearly.
4. Look at these shirts and cuffs which (cuffs) ought to be mended.
5. He laughed at perseverance and enthusiasm, which was foolish and wicked.
6. Those who advise wisely are good friends.

7. All the soldiers began to move, some to the right, others to the left.
8. That is the church they were coming from when the bomb fell.
9. That mountain, whose name I cannot remember, is the highest of the range.
10. Have you seen their little girls, whose cloaks are all of the same colour?
11. My friend, for whom I would do anything, lives there.
12. The stockings which were in the shop window yesterday have been sold.

(*f*) INTERROGATIVE

§ 27. 1. *Quién* is used of persons and *qué*[1] of things.

2. *Cuál*[1] indicates choice between two or more objects and also translates *which? what?* when a part of the verb 'to be' follows.

3. The genitive case must be used to express possession. *Cuyo* (etc.) should not be used. (cf. § 25. 8.)

§ 28. *Examples.*

1. (a) ¿Quiénes son? — Who are they?
   (b) ¿Qué dice ella? — What does she say?
   (c) ¿Qué[1] hora es? — What time is it?
2. (a) ¿Cuál de los billetes desea Vd.? — Which of the tickets do you want?
   (b) ¿Cuál[1] es la fecha? — What is the date?
   (c) ¿Cuáles[1] galletas compraré? — What biscuits shall I buy?
3. ¿De quién era? — Whose was it?

XII. *Translate:*

1. Who suspects me of doing such a thing?
2. What reasons have you and why don't you give them?
3. Which is the train for Seville? That one and it leaves at a quarter to seven.
4. He asked me which of the *mantillas* I thought the prettiest.
5. Whose tickets are these I have found in my overcoat pocket?
6. What does she mean? She speaks French very badly.

1 *Qué* and *cuál* are also Interrogative *Adjectives* corresponding to the French *quel*. For another use of *qué*, *cuál*, cf. § 4. 5.

(g) Miscellaneous

Below are given a number of examples showing the use of the common miscellaneous and indefinite pronouns.

§ 29. *Examples.*

1. Alguien.
   ¿Ha encontrado Vd. a alguien?   Have you met anyone?
2. Alguno. (cf. § 15. 4.)
   Algunos hablaron muy bien.   Some spoke very well.
3. Algo[1].
   (*a*) Nos ofrecían algo.   They were offering us something.
   (*b*) Me falta algo (de) sólido.   I want something solid.
4. Nadie.
   (*a*) No conozco a nadie como él.   I don't know anyone like him.
   (*b*) Nadie se movió de su asiento.   No one moved from his seat.
5. Nada.
   (*a*) La niña no bebió nada.   The little girl didn't drink anything.
   (*b*) Nada bueno resultará de eso.   Nothing good will come of it.
6. Cada uno.
   Distribuyó flores a cada una.   He distributed flowers to each lady.
7. Otro. (cf. § 3. 6.)
   Había otros de quienes no necesito hablar.   There were others of whom I need not speak.
8. Quienquiera.
   A quienesquiera que tengan hambre yo daré alimento.   To whomsoever are hungry I will give food.

XIII. *Translate:*

1. Anyone will give us fruit and milk if we ask for them.
2. There is nothing to eat! What a pity!
3. Three of my aunts will come to-day. I have to give a present to each.
4. Someone has been here; there are foot-marks on the carpet.
5. Whoever writes before the 20th of June will be given seats.
6. Have you lost your fan? I will give you another.

1 *Algo* is also used as an Adverb meaning 'rather.'

CHAPTER V

THE VERB

(a) SUBJECT AND OBJECT

§ **30.** Before entering on a detailed treatment it is necessary to call attention to the following four peculiarities of Spanish verb-construction, which are of primary importance.

These are:

1. The omission, if desired, of the subject pronoun. (cf. § 18. 1.)
2. Inversion of the subject and verb in all sentences if desired and always in interrogative clauses.
3. The use of the Dative case for the direct personal or personified object except after *tener*.
4. Use of the third person plural (as in English) to express an indefinite subject as an alternative to *se* with the third person singular.

§ **31.** *Examples.*

1. (a) Eché la piedra; cayó ruidosamente. — I threw the stone; it fell noisily.
   (b) Pase, caballero, y siéntese. — Come in, sir, and sit down.
2. (a) Era Pedro un hombre grueso. — Peter was a fat man.
   (b) Sonaron las campanas. — The bells rang.
   (c) ¿Cuándo estará bueno su primo? — When will your cousin be well?
   (d) ¿Porqué lo desea ella? — Why does she want it?
   (e) ¿Juega Esteban? — Is Stephen playing?
3. (a) Mirábamos al muchacho. — We were looking at the boy.
   (b) Los paisanos a quienes los perros atacaron. — The peasants whom the dogs attacked.
   (c) ¿Quiere Vd. visitar (a) Madrid? — Do you want to visit Madrid?
   (d) Tuvo una sobrina con él. — He had a niece with him.
4. Dicen en Londres que no habrá elecciones. — They say in London that there will not be an election.

(b) Agreement

§ 32. 1. The verb agrees in person and number with the subject.

2. If the subject is compound containing two or more persons the verb agrees in person with the pronoun which would be used to express all the persons.

§ 33. *Examples.*

1. (*a*) Los toros avanzaron hacia la ciudad.

The bulls advanced toward the city.

  (*b*) Soy yo (yo soy); no son ellos.

It is I; it is not they.

2. (*a*) Vd. y yo les hablaremos.

You and I will speak to them.

  (*b*) Él y ellos salieron.

He and they went out.

XIV. *Translate:*

1. We will go to our rooms now; they are ready for us.
2. In the farmyard the oxen were lowing; the pigs were grunting; thousands of flies were stinging them.
3. Why was this coal sent? It is more expensive than the other.
4. Did the bees make all the honey you wanted?
5. He will judge the prisoner with great severity.
6. The man he shot was another spy.
7. The more I visit Paris, the noisier it appears to be.
8. They had three children, whose names were Elizabeth, Mary and Peter.
9. They say the ghost-train passes through this station every year.
10. She and her mother offended me very much.

(c) Auxiliaries

§ 34. 1. The verb *estar* is used to express situation and temporary or accidental qualities whereas the verb *ser* denotes essential and permanent qualities[1].

2. The verb *haber* is used to form compound tenses of all verbs.

3. The verb *tener* is used in certain expressions in place of the verbs *ser* and *estar*.

[1] These verbs will be referred to again later on.

4. The verb *haber* with *de* and *que* and the verb *tener* with *que* express obligation, the former in a modified sense.
5. The following verbs are found as auxiliaries in place of the verbs *ser* and *estar*: *ir, andar, quedar, hallarse, encontrarse, mostrarse.* They should be used in moderation.
6. The verbs *deber, poder* and *saber* are used as auxiliaries.
7. The English auxiliaries 'do,' 'does,' 'did,' as used in questions have no counterpart in Spanish. (cf. § 31. 2.)

§ 35. *Examples.*

1. (*a*) El Prado está en Madrid. — The Prado is in Madrid.
   (*b*) El Prado es un museo. — The Prado is a museum.
   (*c*) El vaso está vacío. — The glass is empty.
   (*d*) El vaso es pequeño. — The glass is small.
   (*e*) Era pálido después del accidente. — He was pale after the accident.
   (*f*) Era un hombre pálido. — He was a pale man.
2. (*a*) Sin duda lo habrán visto. — Without doubt they will have seen it.
   (*b*) Se han lavado las manos. — They have washed their hands.
3. (*a*) En Madrid tengo mucho frío y mucho calor. — In Madrid I am very cold and very hot.
   (*b*) ¿Cuántos años tiene ella? — How old is she?
   (*c*) Hace calor. Tendremos sed. — It is hot. We shall be thirsty.
   (*d*) No tenga miedo; ¿no tiene vergüenza de mostrarlo? — Don't have any fear. Aren't you ashamed to show it?
4. (*a*) Hay que llegar cuanto antes. — It is necessary to arrive as soon as possible.
   (*b*) Han de dejarnos la semana próxima. — They are to leave us next week.
   (*c*) Tuvo que firmar el documento. — He had to sign the document.
5. (*a*) Iba yo subiendo la colina. — I was climbing the hill.
   (*b*) Andábamos silenciosos. — We were (went along) silent.
   (*c*) Quedan olvidados mis zapatos. — My shoes have been forgotten.

(*d*) Hallóse en un campo dilatado. — He was in an extensive field.

(*e*) Me encontré en la iglesia. — I was in the church.

(*f*) El mar se mostraba tranquilo. — The sea was calm.

6. (*a*) Yo debo escribir. — I must (I ought to) write.

(*b*) Vd. debía haber escrito. — You were to have written.

(*c*) Debieron escribir. — They ought to have written.

(*d*) Debe haber escrito. — He must have (he ought to have) written.

(*e*) He debido escribir. — I have had to write (I must have written).

(*f*) Deberemos escribir. — We shall have to write.

(*g*) Deberían escribir. — They would have to write.

(*h*) Deben llegar hoy. — They (probably) arrive to-day.

(*i*) Puedo ir. — I may go.

(*j*) Él podía (podría) ir. — He might go.

(*k*) Podemos haber ido. — We may have gone.

(*l*) Podrían haber ido. — They might have gone.

(*m*) Vd. ha podido ir. — You have been able to go.

(*n*) Habría podido ir. — I would (might) have been able to go.

(*o*) No sabe nadar. — He doesn't know how to swim.

7. (*a*) ¿Desea él mi firma? — Does he want my signature?

(*b*) ¿Arregló Juan la cuenta? — Did John settle the bill?

XV. *Translate:*

1. Good actors are always industrious.
2. A Catholic priest will be here immediately.
3. Old age is happier when it is free from care.
4. My neighbour has been ill; he is now better.
5. Has the boy finished his Spanish exercise?
6. The cook was so sleepy that she could not prepare our evening meal.
7. The waiter was only twenty-five when he bought his own restaurant.
8. That peasant is tired, cold and hungry. Can you give him something hot to eat?
9. My field and yours are to be sold on August 1st.

10. The sheep, which the shepherd had to look for, has been found.
11. When he heard that, he was silent.
12. He was astonished when I spoke to him.
13. The pretty Italian village through which we passed lies in a sheltered valley.
14. Your governess should teach you geography every day.
15. The soap may be in the bathroom.
16. It had not rained for a long time. The flowers might be dead.
17. I have not been able to paint the picture this month.
18. Spoilt children don't know how to amuse themselves.
19. Do your gardeners work hard in the winter?
20. Does the road go uphill all the way?

(d) Passive Voice

§ 36. 1. The verb *ser* is used to form the Passive Voice.

2. The Passive, when the agent is not expressed, is less used in Spanish than in English, *se* with the Active being frequently employed.

3. The English 'by' after a passive is translated by *por* when the agent is a living being and by *de* when emotion, feeling or a figurative meaning is indicated.

4. The Past Participle in compound tenses (formed with *ser*) always agrees with the subject.

§ 37. *Examples.*

1. La madre fué matada por su hija. — The mother was killed by her daughter.
2. (a) Se llevó arriba el cuerpo. — The body was carried upstairs.
   (b) Se habla inglés. — English is spoken. (cf. § 19. 2.)
   (c) Aquí se venden (los) libros. — Books are sold here.
3. (a) El hoyo fué llenado por el jardinero. — The hole was filled in by the gardener.
   (b) Es querida de sus padres. — She is loved by her parents.
4. (a) La música será compuesta este año. — The music will be composed this year.
   (b) Cinco butacas han sido tomadas. — Five stalls have been taken.

(e) Reflexive Verbs

§ 38. 1. Some verbs are always reflexive[1]; but the majority are only reflexive when the sense demands it.

2. The reflexive pronoun, like the personal pronoun (cf. § 18. 4), always follows the Infinitive, Present Participle and Affirmative Commands. It *may* follow the third singular and plural in tenses for the sake of style. This use is not common, is limited to the Present, Imperfect and Preterite Indicative, and the verb must stand at the beginning of the clause.

3. A few verbs take on a more intensive or modified meaning when employed reflexively.

4. In Affirmative Commands the first person plural loses the final *s* of the verb and the second person plural (familiar) the final *d*.

5. The Past Participle never agrees in reflexive verbs.

§ 39. *Examples.*

1.	(a) Se quejan del clima.	They complain of the climate.
	(b) Me jacto de mis riquezas.	I boast of my riches.
	(c) Nos levantamos a las ocho.	We get up at eight.
	(d) La puerta se abrió.	The door opened.
2.	(a) Va a casarse con él.	She is going to marry him.
	(b) Aprovechándome del buen tiempo, partí.	Taking advantage of the fine weather, I started.
	(c) Enojábase el cura.	The priest got angry.
3.	(a) Se comieron las frutas.	They ate up the fruit.
	(b) El anciano se muere.	The old man is dying.
	(c) Nos fuimos de prisa.	We went away quickly.
4.	(a) Sentémonos con Vd.	Let us sit with you.
	(b) Levantáos, caballeros.	Rise, gentlemen.
5.	(a) Ella se ha matado.	She has killed herself.
	(b) Los amigos se han encontrado.	The friends have met.

1 *Abstenerse*; *arrepentirse*; *atreverse*; *jactarse*; *quejarse*.

XVI. *Translate:*

1. The officers will be elected by the king and his ministers.
2. Boots and shoes are often cleaned in the streets in Spain.
3. Passengers are requested to leave their luggage at the Customs.
4. My socks were mended at home by my housekeeper.
5. Do you know Ávila, that old city surrounded by huge walls?
6. Comfortable offices have been built by the government.
7. The dog repented of what he had done, and asked pardon!
8. The more he abstained from vice, the stronger he grew.
9. They married last year and are living in the country.
10. It is not wise to deceive oneself.
11. He found me looking at myself in the glass.
12. My brother-in-law will have gone away before to-morrow.
13. He drank off a glass of red wine.
14. Let us have breakfast now; it is eight o'clock.
15. Wash, children, and brush your hair.
16. My affection for him has changed into hatred.

(*f*) Impersonal Verbs

§ 40. Below are given examples of the employment of some Impersonal Verbs and expressions.

§ 41. *Examples.*

(*a*) Llueve mucho ahora.	It is raining heavily now.
(*b*) Ha helado mucho en la noche.	It froze a lot in the night.
(*c*) Parece que tendremos truenos.	It looks as though we shall have thunder.
(*d*) No puedo hallar la llave. No importa.	I can't find the key. It doesn't matter.
(*e*) Nos faltan plumas.	We need pens.
(*f*) Hay un ladrón en la casa.	There is a robber in the house.
(*g*) Había postres en la mesa.	There were sweet biscuits on the table.
(*h*) Hubo una tempestad ayer.	There was a storm yesterday.
(*i*) Habrá mucho que ver.	There will be much to see.
(*j*) Ha habido una gran nevada.	There has been a great fall of snow.

(k) Hacía sol en el sur.	It was sunny in the south.
(l) Yo estuve en Málaga hace diez años.	I was in Malaga ten years ago.
(m) Hace cinco días que llegué.	It's five days since I came.
(n) Nos gusta la música.	We like music.
(o) No le gustan las naranjas.	He doesn't like oranges.
(p) Hay que preguntar siempre.	It is always necessary to ask. (cf. § 34. 4.)
(q) Amaneció a las cuatro; anocheció a las siete.	It dawned at four o'clock, it got dark at seven.
(r) Es lástima que no vengan.	It is a pity that they don't come.
(s) Es de esperar que la guerra se acabe pronto.	It is to be hoped that the war will end soon.

XVII. *Translate:*

1. It was snowing when we left London yesterday.
2. It is very important to write clearly.
3. It happened that it was raining whilst we were inside.
4. It will be necessary to take brushes, combs and towels.
5. It is beautifully fine to-day. Will you come with me to the sea?
6. They suspected me of this ten days ago.
7. There will have been many visitors during our absence.
8. I shall want a pillow during this long journey.
9. I don't like braces: I always wear a belt.
10. It is evident that no one will come.

(g) INDICATIVE MOOD

§ 42. *The Present:*

1. Takes the place of the English perfect in continuous action.
2. Makes a narrative more graphic.
3. Is used after *si* in conditional clauses.
4. May be formed by *estar* with the present participle[1].

[1] To express continuous action. Similarly in § 44. 4, § 48. 1, § 50. 4, § 52. 2, § 54. 2.

§ 43. *Examples.*

1. (*a*) Estamos aquí desde (hace) una semana.
   We have been here a week.

   (*b*) Hace dos horas que me mira.
   He has been looking at me for two hours.

2. Llaman, entran, le hallan muerto.
   They knocked, went in and found him dead.

3. Si Vd. pierde esto, no le daré otro.
   If you lose this, I shall not give you another.

4. Estamos trabajando seriamente.
   We are working seriously.

§ 44. *The Imperfect:*

1. Expresses *habit, custom* or *state.*
2. Takes the place of the English pluperfect in continuous action.
3. Is used after *si* in conditional clauses.
4. May be formed by *estar* with the present participle.

§ 45. *Examples.*

1. (*a*) Pensaba muchas veces en mi madre.
   I often used to think of my mother.

   (*b*) Me despertaban con mucho ruido.
   They used to wake me with much noise.

   (*c*) La pobre era ciega.
   The poor woman was blind.

2. (*a*) Estaban un año en la escuela cuando se cerró.
   They had been a year in the school when it shut.

   (*b*) Hacía un año que trabajábamos.
   We had been working for a year.

3. Si tenía virtudes, tenía faltas también.
   If he had virtues, he had faults also.

4. Ella estaba tocando el piano.
   She was playing the piano.

§ 46. *The Preterite:*

1. Expresses a completed action in past time.
2. When used in conjunction with the Imperfect it expresses the shorter of two actions.

3. Is generally used for the Past tense in ordinary conversation.

4. May be used instead of the Imperfect in conditional clauses. (cf. § 44. 3.)

§ 47. *Examples.*

1. El ejército luchó todo el día y ganó la batalla.	The army struggled all day and won the battle.
2. Yo escribía en mi despacho cuando entró.	I was writing in my office when he came in.
3. Busqué al cartero y al fin le hallé.	I looked for the postman and at last found him.
4. Si logró debe ser un hombre hábil.	If he succeeded he must be a clever man.

§ 48. *The Perfect:*

May be formed by *estar* with the present participle.

§ 49. *Examples.*

He estado leyendo en la biblioteca.	I have been reading in the library.

§ 50. *The Pluperfect:*

1. When formed with *había* expresses the English *had* without qualification.

2. When formed with *hube* is used after certain conjunctions of time and gives the idea of immediate action[1].

3. May be expressed by the Preterite[2].

4. May be formed by *estar* with the present participle.

§ 51. *Examples.*

1. Yo lo había arreglado.	I had arranged it.
2. (*a*) Apenas hubieron dicho eso cuando entré.	Hardly had they said that when I came in.
(*b*) Luego que hube leído el papel lo quemé.	As soon as I had read the paper I burnt it.
(*c*) No bien hubo acabado de hablar que empezó a llover.	No sooner had he finished speaking than it began to rain.

1 This distinction is not observed strictly.　　2 Rarely used.

3. Apenas se ocultó[1] comenzaron a hablar.

He had scarcely hidden himself when they began to talk.

4. Habían estado viviendo dos meses con nosotros.

They had been living two months with us.

§ 52. *The Future and Future Perfect:*

1. Express probability in present and past time respectively.

2. May be formed by *estar* with the present participle, though rarely in the case of the Future Perfect.

§ 53. *Examples.*

1. (*a*) Serán las nueve y media.

It is about half-past nine.

   (*b*) Lo habrá negado.

He probably denied it.

2. (*a*) Estaré esperando al carpintero a mediodía.

I shall be expecting the carpenter at twelve.

   (*b*) Habremos estado corriendo una media hora.

We shall have been running half an hour.

§ 54. *The Conditional and Past Conditional:*

1. Express probability in past time.

2. May be formed by *estar* with the present participle, though rarely in the case of the Past Conditional.

3. Often take the form of the Imperfect Subjunctive in *ra*.

§ 55. *Examples.*

1. (*a*) Sería en el mes de Julio cuando sucedió.

It was probably in the month of July that it happened.

   (*b*) Entonces se habría quedado sordo.

He had become deaf about then.

2. (*a*) Estarían fumando si tuviesen tabaco.

They would be smoking if they had tobacco.

   (*b*) Yo me habría estado contentándome con menos, si no hubiese deseado más.

I would have been content with less, if I had not wanted more.

3. Ví la casa que me hubiera convenido.

I saw the house which would have suited me.

1 Rarely used.

XVIII. *Translate:*

1. He has slept now for ten hours.
2. May I introduce my brother to you? I have known him for a long time.
3. He approached quietly, raised his gun, fired and ran away.
4. If you open that box to-morrow, you will find something valuable in it.
5. Where is James? He is smoking in the library.
6. For many years a hundred men slept in this small room.
7. The frog was so fat that it almost burst.
8. We had been playing half an hour when it began to rain.
9. The priest raised his hands and blessed the soldiers.
10. I killed the fly which was buzzing round my head.
11. The child entered the post office and bought a dozen stamps.
12. If they proved that, they will be pardoned.
13. The choir has made progress since the beginning of the year.
14. The cathedral bells have been ringing; now they have stopped.
15. As soon as the news had been announced, everyone rushed into the streets.
16. The jeweller had brought the necklace from his shop to our house.
17. We had been talking about that.
18. Your pocket-book is probably in your coat pocket.
19. Some of the letters may have arrived the day before yesterday; the rest, to-day.
20. It was about midnight when a fearful noise was heard.
21. I don't know if he would do that now.
22. That waiter would be serving us, if he were not (*subj.*) so lazy.

(*h*) IMPERATIVE MOOD

§ 56. 1. The pronoun-subject, familiar and formal, may be omitted but the formal *Vd.*, *Vds.* should be included if the Imperative only occurs once and in other cases should be included with the first of two or more Imperatives. (cf. § 18. 1.)

2. The pronoun-object (*a*) follows the Imperative affirmative and is written as one word with it, the appropriate accent being added, and (*b*) precedes the Imperative negative. (cf. § 18. 4.)

3. The Present Subjunctive is used for the negative of the familiar Imperative.

§ 57. *Examples.*

1. (*a*) Aprende (tu) la lección de francés.

    Learn the French lesson.

    (*b*) Un señor acaba de llegar. Que pase.

    A gentleman has just arrived. Let him come in.

    (*c*) Calle Vd.; el telón va a levantarse.

    Be quiet; the curtain is going up.

    (*d*) Llamen Vds., entren y pregunten por ella.

    Knock, go in and ask for her.

2. (*a*) Déjame gustar el vino.

    Let me taste the wine.

    (*b*) Ofrézcanoslos Vd. alguna vez.

    Offer them to us sometimes.

    (*c*) No le quite (Vd.) su sobretodo.

    Don't take away his overcoat from him.

3. (*a*) Dáselo a él; no nos lo des.

    Give it to him; don't give it to us.

    (*b*) Tirad por aquí, no tiréis por allí.

    Pull this way, don't pull that way.

XIX. *Translate*[1]:

1. Collect the books and put them here.
2. There are some dirty beggars at the door. Let them wait.
3. Follow me. The bedrooms are in another part of the house.
4. Do not write more letters than you are able.
5. Don't show yourself a coward in front of danger.

(*i*) INFINITIVE MOOD

§ 58. The Infinitive is used:

1. As a substantive in place of the English substantive or gerund. (cf. § 1.)
2. As an equivalent to an Imperative in formal use.
3. In the place of a subordinate clause when the subordinate and principal clauses have the same subject.

[1] *Put the Commands into Formal and Familiar form.*

4. Instead of the English Gerund after prepositions.

5. Without a preposition after *querer, poder, saber, lograr*, and many other verbs.

6. With *a* after *ir, venir, empezar, comenzar, invitar, enseñar, aprender*.

7. With *de* after nouns, and generally after adjectives and certain verbs.

8. With *en* after *lograr, pensar*.

9. As subordinate verb, active or passive, without a preposition after *hacer, mandar, dejar, ver, entender*.

10. With *al* for the English Gerund.

11. With *a no* in place of a negative conditional clause.

§ 59. *Examples.*

1. El reir es saludable.	Laughing is healthy.
2. No fumar: Ver las reglamentos.	No smoking: See Regulations.
3. (*a*) Siento haberlo visto.	I am sorry that I saw it.
(*b*) Él creía hacerlo mañana.	He thought he would do it to-morrow.
4. (*a*) Después de viajar mucho vivió en Londres.	After travelling a good deal he lived in London.
(*b*) Antes de desayunarme me paseo.	Before breakfasting I go for a walk.
(*c*) Marchó sin pagar nada.	He went away without paying anything.
(*d*) Vd. gasta su tiempo en leer libros estúpidos.	You waste your time reading stupid books.
5. (*a*) Quisiera ponerme las botas.	I should like to put on my boots.
(*b*) ¿No puede Vd. alabarle de vez en cuando?	Cannot you praise him now and then?
(*c*) Sabían hablar ruso.	They knew how to speak Russian.
(*d*) Logró aprender el italiano.	He succeeded in learning Italian.

6. (*a*) Vaya Vd. a buscar al cochero.

Go and look for the coachman.

   (*b*) Empezaron a llorar amargamente.

They began to weep bitterly.

7. (*a*) Su manera de pensar me extraña.

His way of thinking astonishes me.

   (*b*) Estoy curioso de saber porqué.

I am curious to know why.

   (*c*) Acabaron de escribir hace poco.

They finished writing a short time ago.

   (*d*) Acaban de dar las once.

Eleven o'clock has just struck.

   (*e*) Trataré de venir el jueves.

I will try to come on Thursday.

   (*f*) No olvide Vd. (de) escribirme.

Don't forget to write to me.

8. Pienso en quedar aquí.

I am thinking of remaining here.

9. (*a*) Hizo (mandó) construir una casa.

He had a house built.

   (*b*) Ella se dejó engañar.

She allowed herself to be cheated.

   (*c*) Ví entrar al rey.

I saw the king come in.

   (*d*) ¿Oyó Vd. cantar el ruiseñor?

Did you hear the nightingale sing?

10. Al entrar en la tienda pidió un periódico.

Entering the shop he asked for a paper.

11. A no ser tarde volvería yo a leerlo.

If it were not late I would read it again.

XX. *Translate:*

1. He told me that crossing the road outside his house was dangerous.
2. I deny that I saw it; I assert that you and your friend saw it.
3. He put the things away without breaking anything.
4. Everyone must knock before coming into the office.
5. The sailor wanted to show us the lighthouse.
6. Cats can sleep profoundly at any time.
7. The pilot will know how to take us out of the harbour.
8. My lawyer came and saw my estate some time ago.
9. After seeing the candlesticks he went and bought them.
10. It is beginning to snow; let us run home quickly.
11. It was he who taught me to love drawing.
12. That method of counting is strange and interesting.

13. It is foolish to abandon a game when you begin to lose.
14. The major consented to come to the ball.
15. The allied generals think of attacking to-morrow at dawn.
16. The Prime Minister's secretary will have the paper signed this afternoon.
17. We saw that woman strike the child.
18. I am going to see the policeman who heard the man ask for help.
19. On opening the study door, the servant noticed a strong smell of gas.
20. If it were not too early, I should start for the station now.

(*j*) THE PARTICIPLES

§ 60. *The Present Participle:*

1. Is invariable, and never used as an adjective.
2. Is replaced by the Infinitive after verbs of *seeing* and *hearing.* (cf. § 60. 8.)
3. May be replaced by a relative clause.
4. May have the personal pronoun to avoid ambiguity or for euphony.
5. Is complementary to the verbs *estar, ir, seguir, andar* and *quedar*, etc.: used as auxiliaries. (cf. § 34. 5.)
6. Is written as one word with the personal pronoun it governs, with the appropriate accent. (cf. § 20. 4.)

§ 61. *Examples.*

1. (*a*) Saltando del muro escaparon. — Jumping from the wall they escaped.
   (*b*) Llevando sus joyas brillantes. — Wearing her shining jewels.
   (*c*) En el jardín había unas flores encantadoras. — In the garden were some charming flowers.
2. (*a*) Miramos entrar los buques. — We saw the ships entering.
   (*b*) ¿Oyó Vd. gritar al niño? — Did you hear the child cry out?

3. (a) Nos gustan las ventanas que dan a la calle.

We like windows looking on to the street.

(b) Escuchábamos los lobos que aullaban.

We were listening to the wolves howling.

4. Ocupando yo esta silla, Vd. debe hallar otra.

As I have this chair, you must find another.

5. (a) El toro estaba pastando la yerba (or hierba).

The bull was eating the grass.

(b) El hombre iba corriendo.

The man was running.

(c) Todo el mundo seguía trabajando.

Everyone went on working.

(d) Anda haciendo errores.

He goes on making mistakes.

(e) Quedé leyendo toda la tarde.

I read the whole afternoon.

6. Invitándome para mañana se despidió.

Inviting me for to-morrow he took his leave.

§ 62. *The Past Participle:*

1. Is invariable in the Active voice.
2. Agrees with the subject in the Passive.
3. Agrees as an adjective with the subject after an auxiliary verb.

§ 63. *Examples.*

1. (a) La carta que he escrito es para mi sobrino.

The letter I have written is to my nephew.

(b) Ella se ha vestido rápidamente.

She has dressed quickly.

(c) Habían presenciado la pieza.

They had been present at the play.

2. (a) La leche ha sido bebida por él.

The milk has been drunk by him.

(b) Aquellas peras deben ser comidas.

Those pears ought to be eaten.

3. (a) El agua está helada.

The water is frozen.

(b) Estaban acostados en la hierba.

They were lying on the grass.

XXI. *Translate:*

1. The girls, trembling with fear, fled from the growling animal.
2. I found my nephew reading a most interesting book.
3. The bull saw the *matador* approaching and rushed towards him.
4. We watched the amusing actor making everyone laugh.
5. Since *they* advise this, what more can *I* say?
6. The woman was sweeping the steps leading up to the front door.
7. The water is subsiding rapidly.
8. That troublesome owl went on hooting all night.
9. He offered me wine, pouring it into a pale-green wine glass.
10. The date he has arranged is May the 15th.
11. Hundreds of people have interested themselves in his affairs.
12. The stars have been observed by astronomers for many centuries.
13. The lazy girls were sitting there doing nothing.
14. The rose is withered; throw it into the fire.

(k) SUBJUNCTIVE MOOD

§ 64. In general: The Subjunctive is used in subordinate clauses to express doubt or uncertainty, and depends for its use *either* on the verb of the principal clause *or*, in adverbial clauses, on the conjunction introducing the subordinate clause *or*, in adjectival clauses, on the character of its antecedent.

In particular: The Subjunctive is used:

1. After a principal verb expressing *wish, command*[1], *prohibition*[1], *permission*[1], *emotion, doubt*, and *fear*.
2. In relative clauses when the antecedent is indefinite.
3. After Indefinite *Pronouns, Adjectives*, and *Adverbs*.
4. After certain impersonal verbs and expressions, not expressing certainty.
5. After *cuando* in a subordinate clause when reference is to the future.

1 These verbs may be followed by the Infinitive.

6. After *si* when the statement is contrary to fact or expectation.

7. After *aunque* (even if), *para que, sin que, con tal que, hasta que* (with reference to the future), *a menos que, como si.*

8. In a few principal clauses used as exclamations.

§ 65. *Examples.*

1. (a) Quiero que él estudie más.	I want him to study more.
(b) Mandaron que se vendiese la casa.	They gave orders that the house should be sold.
Mandaron vender la casa.	
(c) Diremos al mendigo que se vaya.	We will tell the beggar to go away.
Diremos al mendigo irse.	
(d) (Le) prohibo que Vd. entre.	I forbid your coming in.
No (le) permito entrar.	
(e) Sentirán que Vds. no hayan escrito.	They will be sorry that you haven't written.
(f) Dudábamos que viviese.	We were doubtful if he would live.
(g) ¿Teme Vd. que yo se lo diga?	Are you afraid that I shall tell him?
2. Busco a un muchacho que (quien) me guíe.	I am looking for a boy to guide me.
3. (a) Quienquiera que no pague quedará fuera.	Whoever does not pay will stop outside.
(b) Haga Vd. cualquier cosa que sea buena.	Whatever is good, do it.
(c) Cualesquiera libros que compre los leeré.	Whatever books I buy I shall read.
(d) Él me seguirá dondequiera que yo vaya.	He will follow me wherever I go.
(e) Por más pobres que sean viven bien.	However poor they are they live well.
(f) Por sagaz que fuese su plan, fracasó.	However wise his plan was, it failed.

4. (a) Importa que vengan pronto. — It is important that they should come soon.

(b) Parecía que lo hubiese tomado. — It seemed that he had taken it.

(c) Es posible que muera. — It is possible that he will die.

(d) Bastará que dos hablen. — It will be enough for two to speak.

5. (a) Cuando yo llame, abra Vd. — When I knock, open.

(b) Decidiré cuando hayan contestado. — I will decide when they have answered.

6. (a) Yo le prestaría dinero si lo tuviese. — I would lend you money if I had it.

(b) Si no hubiésemos subido, él hubiera bajado. — If we hadn't gone up, he would have come down.

7. (a) Aunque estuviese aquí no le vería. — Even if he were here I wouldn't see him.

(b) Me envió para que comprase fruta. — He sent me to buy fruit.

(c) Se fueron sin que yo les hablase. — They went away without my speaking to them.

(d) Con tal que digan la verdad les perdonaré. — Provided that they tell the truth I will forgive them.

(e) Espere Vd. hasta que vengan. — Wait until they come.

(f) La salvaremos a ella a menos que sea demasiado tarde. — We shall save her unless it is too late.

(g) Corrió como si tuviese gran miedo. — He ran as if he were very afraid.

8. Viva España. Viva el rey. — Long live Spain! Long live the king!

XXII. *Translate:*

1. John will want the coffee to be served hot.
2. The German consul ordered him to call at midday.
3. The cow prevented the calf from leaving the field.
4. I am very surprised you have slept well on such a hard bed.
5. Her parents doubt whether she will have an agreeable journey.
6. The baker is afraid that there will not be enough bread for us.

7. I must buy a piece of ribbon to suit this dress.
8. Whoever gets there first shall have the best seats.
9. He will sing whatever songs you give him.
10. Wherever there were few inns the roads were bad.
11. Whatever books he lent[1] me I read.
12. I shall not enjoy my holidays, however long they are.
13. It is certain that thunder follows[1] lightning.
14. It is probable that your canary left its cage, the door of which was open.
15. You must see the garden when the carnations and roses are in flower.
16. If that chicken had more feathers it might live longer.
17. The famous author was unhappy until his last novel was[1] finished.
18. I do not advise you to stop until they come.
19. He fought with the animal without our helping him.
20. Their pictures will be worth a lot provided that they are not sold too soon.

§ 66. *Additional Verb Constructions.*

The following constructions, in addition to those that have been dealt with, are amongst those in common use.

(*a*) Volvieron a ofrecérmelo.	They offered it to me again.
(*b*) No tengo nada que ver con eso.	I have nothing to do with that.
(*c*) Busco la carta.	I am looking for the letter.
(*d*) Escucharé la música.	I shall listen to the music.
(*e*) Mirábamos el castillo.	We were looking at the castle.
(*f*) Esperando el tren.	Waiting for the train.
(*g*) Llegó a ser serio.	It became serious.
(*h*) El soldado pensaba en su patria.	The soldier was thinking of his fatherland.
(*i*) Ha cumplido con su deber.	He has done his duty.
(*j*) Casándose con ella se hizo rico.	By marrying her he became rich.
(*k*) ¿Quiere Vd. comprar uno a mi padre?	Will you buy one from my father?
(*l*) Pida Vd. un vaso al mozo.	Ask the waiter for a glass.
(*m*) Me quitaron el bastón.	They took away my stick.

1 *Indicative or subjunctive?*

(n) Dí con él en la plaza. — I met him in the Square.

(o) i. Se puso lívido. — He got pale.

ii. La cocinera se puso a hacer una tortilla. — The cook began to make an omelette.

(p) i. Echaron de ver un objeto curioso. — They noticed a curious object.

ii. Se echó a reir. — He burst out laughing.

(q) (Me) he aprovechado de mi visita. — I have benefited from my visit.

(r) Él sacó su dinero y tomó una peseta. — He took out his money and took a peseta.

(s) i. Acabábamos de lavarnos. — We had just washed.

ii. Acabaron de lavarse. — They finished washing.

(t) ¿Qué fué de ello? — What became of it?

(u) Estoy por viajar este año. — I am in favour of (feel like) travelling this year.

(v) No pude menos de sonreir. — I couldn't help smiling.

(w) i. Dejaré de cantar. — I shall give up (leave off) singing.

ii. No deje Vd. de informarme. — Do not fail to inform me.

(x) Se hizo cargo de ello. — He took note of (paid attention to) it.

(y) No cabe más en la sala. — There is no more room in the hall.

(z) Nos faltan plumas. — We need pens.

CHAPTER VI

THE ADVERB

§ 67. 1. Examples are given below of Adverbs of *Place, Time, Manner, Quantity, Interrogation, Affirmation,* and *Negation.*

2. The Adverb is generally placed before the Adjective and after the Verb qualified, but for the sake of style and euphony it may be placed anywhere in the sentence. Interrogative Adverbs and *apenas* are always placed at the beginning of a clause.

3. A noun with *con* may take the place of an Adverb.

4. When more than one Adverb of similar formation occurs in a sentence the termination *-mente* is generally added to the last only.

5. The Adverbs of negation *nunca, jamás* and *tampoco* must be used with a verb without *no* provided that they are placed before the verb. (cf. § 31.)

6. The English 'only' with a verb may be translated by *no más...que.*

7. The affirmative Adverb *sí* has an elegant use and practically takes the place of an Emphatic English verb.

8. The Adverb *ya* has, besides the meaning of 'already,' a number of meanings best understood by observation.

§ 68. *Examples.*

1. (*a*) Hay más gente dentro que fuera.

There are more people inside than outside.

(*b*) Ven acá, Juan; ponte delante.

Come here, John; put yourself in front.

(*c*) Vd. baila a menudo; yo raras veces.

You dance often; I rarely do.

(*d*) Volvieron después muy cansados.

Afterwards, they came back very tired.

(*e*) Por lo tanto trabajó de mala gana. — Therefore he worked unwillingly.

(*f*) Lo copiaré despacio. — I will copy it slowly.

(*g*) Comí mucho, pero no demasiado. — I ate much, but not too much.

(*h*) ¿Cómo hallaré a mi hermano? — How shall I find my brother?

(*i*) ¿De dónde llevaron eso? — Where did they bring that from?

(*j*) Puedo comprender el inglés. Claro[1]. — I can understand English. Evidently.

(*k*) No dijimos ni una palabra. — We didn't say a word.

(*l*) Vd. no me lo ofreció siquiera. — You didn't even offer it me.

2. (*a*) Es extremamente bonita. — She is extremely pretty.

(*b*) Él lo olvidó completamente. — He forgot it completely.

(*c*) Lentamente avanzaba hacia la puerta. — He was moving slowly towards the door.

(*d*) Apenas acabaron a tiempo. — They had hardly finished in time.

(*e*) ¿Porqué me lo pide Vd.? — Why do you ask me for it?

3. Aprende de memoria con facilidad. — He easily learns by heart.

4. El aeroplán descendió rápida y graciosamente. — The aeroplane came down rapidly and gracefully.

5. (*a*) Nunca consentiré *or* No consentiré nunca. — I will never consent.

(*b*) Jamás iré *or* No iré jamás. — I will never go.

(*c*) Ellos tampoco. — Neither do they. (cf. § 29. 4, 5.)

6. No había en el árbol más que seis ciruelas *or* Había en el árbol solamente seis ciruelas. — There were only six plums on the tree.

7. No me gustan naranjas pero sí manzanas. — I don't like oranges but I do like apples.

8. (*a*) El tren está retrasado. Ya viene. — The train is late. Here it comes.

(*b*) Se ha puesto ya el sol. — Now the sun has set.

(*c*) Ya no soy joven. — I am no longer young.

1 *Claro* is a common expression in Spanish for 'of course,' 'certainly,' etc.

XXIII. *Translate:*

1. Solid pieces of ice were floating around.
2. Soon this cupboard underneath will be empty; that one above is full.
3. Wake up quickly; the bell has just rung.
4. That fat man should sleep less and walk more.
5. When will cotton become cheaper here?
6. The races will be at three o'clock; the bullfight will take place afterwards.
7. The moon still rises early; you will be able to walk home.
8. The lights are never put out at night; they are always burning.
9. There are only five rooms on the ground floor.
10. Soldiers do not seek money, but they do seek glory.

CHAPTER VII

THE PREPOSITION

§ 69. Below are given examples of some Prepositions classified under *Time*, *Place*, and *Manner*.

Examples.

§ 70. Time.

(*a*) Despiérteme (Vd.) antes de las seis.	Wake me before six.
(*b*) Ganaré más después de Mayo.	I shall earn more after May.
(*c*) Desde ayer el tiempo se ha mejorado.	Since yesterday the weather has improved.
(*d*) Durante la corrida el calor era sofocante.	During the bullfight the heat was suffocating.
(*e*) Hasta este año fué gran cazador.	Up to (until) this year he was a great hunter.
(*f*) A las dos y cuarto comenzó la partida.	At a quarter past two the game began.
(*g*) Se vió una luz hacia el este.	A light was seen towards the East.
(*h*) Vivieron en ésta por seis días.	They lived in this town for six days.

§ 71. Place.

(*a*) i. Comparecí ante el tribunal.	I appeared before (in the presence of) the tribunal.
ii. Nos aguarda delante del alcázar.	He is waiting for us in front of the alcazar.
(*b*) i. Detrás[1] del teatro hay una fuente.	Behind the theatre there is a fountain.
ii. Tras[1] la vaca corrió el becerro.	After the cow ran the calf.
(*c*) Irá a España para trabajar en Barcelona.	He will go to Spain to work in Barcelona.
(*d*) Más allá de la escuela está el hospital.	Beyond the school is the hospital.

1 *Tras*, *detrás de* and *bajo*, *debajo de* may be used interchangeably.

(e) El perro se lanzó por las calles. — The dog rushed through the streets.

(f) Ella paseaba a través del bosque. — She was walking through (across) the wood.

(g) Había silencio dentro de (en) la iglesia. — There was silence in the church.

(h) Lejos de aquí vive solo. — Far from here he lives alone.

(i) i. Bajo¹ (debajo de¹) los árboles hay sombra agradable. — Under the trees there is pleasant shade.

ii. Pasó la noche bajo pena de muerte. — He spent the night under penalty of death.

(j) Descanse Vd. al lado de mi padre. — Rest at my father's side.

(k) Andaban los ladrones alrededor de la aldea. — The robbers prowled round the village.

(l) Voló (por) encima del (sobre el) tejado. — It flew over the roof.

(m) Sobre (en) la mesa lo hallará Vd. — You will find it on the table.

(n) i. El paraguas cayó entre la silla y la pared. — The umbrella fell between the chair and the wall.

ii. Hubo un traidor entre ellos. — There was a traitor amongst them.

(o) El buzón está enfrente de la esquina. — The letter box is opposite the corner.

§ 72. Manner.

(a) i. A pesar de la lluvia salimos. — In spite of the rain we went out.

ii. Lo creyó a pesar nuestro. — He believed it in spite of us.

(b) i. Daré dos pesetas por aquel libro. — I will give two pesetas for that book.

ii. Don Quijote fué escrito por Cervantes. — Don Quixote was written by Cervantes.

(c) He aquí una carta para Vd. — Here is a letter for you.

(d) Se muestra generoso para con ella. — He is generous towards her.

1 *Tras, detrás de* and *bajo, debajo de* may be used interchangeably.

(e) Pagaremos el tres de enero. — We will pay on the third of January.

(f) Hasta su hermano lo admite. — Even his brother admits it.

(g) Todos irán excepto (menos) yo. — All will go except me.

(h) Obró según mi consejo. — He acted according to my advice.

(i) Vivía con riquezas pero sin amigos. — He lived with wealth but without friends.

(j) i. Perdí mi reloj de oro. — I lost my gold watch.

ii. Era una hermosa mañana de otoño. — It was a lovely autumn morning.

iii. Quiere a su madre con todo su corazón. — He loves his mother with all his heart.

iv. Lleno de gozo, prosiguió su camino. — Filled with joy, he continued on his road.

v. Continuaron su viaje a pie. — They continued their journey on foot.

(k) El señor de la triste figura. — The gentleman with the sad countenance.

(l) Compramos tres billetes de a cinco pesetas. — We bought three five peseta tickets.

XXIV. *Translate:*

1. For half-an-hour he made careful notes.
2. It is very pleasant to wander through a foreign country.
3. The ambassador went to Italy and stayed in Rome.
4. I hid my face behind my handkerchief.
5. These laces are for the blind man; he will receive a little money for them.
6. Shall we rest under that splendid elm-tree?
7. The dog, tired and weak with hunger, dropped at my feet.
8. Before one o'clock the car appeared before the house.
9. Both travellers had to continue their journey on horseback.
10. Please give me ten $2\frac{1}{2}d$. stamps.

CHAPTER VIII

THE CONJUNCTION

§ 73. 1. Below are given examples of common simple and compound conjunctions, excluding those of § 65. 8.

2. *Y* (and) becomes *e* before a word beginning with *i, hi*. It is not used so extensively as in English[1].

O (or) becomes *u* before a word beginning with *o* or *ho*.

3. 'But' after a negative is *sino*.

§ 74. *Examples.*

1. (*a*) He estudiado la novela clásica y moderna.
I have studied the classic and modern novel.

(*b*) Me gusta el estilo heroico o romántico.
I like the classical or romantic style.

(*c*) Nos saludó pero (mas) no se paró.
He bowed to us but did not stop.

(*d*) Ni mi hermano ni yo podíamos ayudar.
Neither I nor my brother was able to help.

(*e*) Un día que me hallaba con él me habló de su vida.
One day when I was with him he spoke to me of his life.

(*f*) Mientras (que) él hablaba me adormecí.
Whilst he was speaking I went to sleep.

(*g*) Abrí la puerta luego que sonó el timbre.
As soon as the bell rang I opened the door.

(*h*) Lo quemé porque era inútil.
I burnt it because it was useless.

(*i*) Desde que ella murió él no ha salido.
Since she died he has not been out.

(*j*) Después de desnudarme me acosté.
After taking off my clothes I went to bed

(*k*) Nos soportaron de modo que (de suerte que, de manera que) pudimos seguir.
They supported us so that we were able to go on.

1 I.e. a number of clauses connected by 'and' in English would be connected in Spanish by a comma or semi-colon, the 'and' being omitted.

(*l*) i. Esto tiene que concluir sea ahora sea más tarde. — It is to be finished whether now or later.

ii. Escoja Vd. o la paz o la guerra. — Choose either peace or war.

iii. Ya (ora) este niño ya (ora) aquél me tormenta. — Now this child now that one worries me.

(*m*) i. Así (la) Francia como (la) Inglaterra son amigas de España. — Both France and England are friends of Spain.

ii. Los puercos así como las gallinas se han escapado. — The pigs as well as the hens have escaped.

(*n*) Pues, una mañana me dijo la verdad. — Well, one morning he told me the truth.

2. (*a*) Padre e hijo vinieron a encontrarme. — Father and son came to meet me.

(*b*) Verano e invierno el anciano tiene un fuego. — Summer and winter the old man has a fire.

(*c*) Tuvo siete u ocho tiendas. — He had seven or eight shops.

(*d*) Fué herido en el brazo u hombro. — He was wounded in the arm or shoulder.

(*e*) Llamó a la puerta, entró con estrépito. — He knocked at the door, and noisily entered.

3. (*a*) No lo hice yo sino Vd. — I didn't do it; you did.

(*b*) No era ayer sino anteayer que sucedió. — It wasn't yesterday but the day before that it happened.

XXV. *Translate:*

1. Do you prefer silver or gold?
2. Steel and iron are metals.
3. The sun does not lie to the east but to the west of us.
4. The dining-room is not large, but[1] it is comfortable.
5. Travel in the spring instead of in the winter.
6. Although the school was shut we were able to visit it.
7. Now that the peaches are ripe they can be picked.
8. The portrait was hung opposite the window, so that it could be seen in a good light.

1 *Sino* or *pero*?

CHAPTER IX

DIMINUTIVES AND AUGMENTATIVES

§ 75. It is not easy to say precisely when and how Diminutives and Augmentatives should be used in Composition[1]. The only safe course to take is to study carefully their employment by modern authors. Diminutives are more frequent than Augmentatives.

Diminutives:

1. in *-ito, -cito, -ecito* referring to *size* only may be freely employed.
2. in *-ito, -cito, -ecito* indicating *affection* and in *-uelo, -zuelo, -ezuelo* indicating *depreciation* should be used with moderation.
3. in *-ito, -cito, -ecito* found in parts of speech other than nouns should be rarely employed.

Augmentatives:

4. in *-ón, -azo* indicate *size* with or without *depreciation,* and *action* of a noun.
5. in *-ote, -acho, -ucho* indicate *depreciation* with or without reference to *size.*

§ 76. *Examples.*

1. (*a*) Un chiquito de cinco años.	An urchin five years old.
(*b*) No hay más que un jardincito.	There is only a small garden.
(*c*) Mira aquella lucecita.	Look at that little light.
2. (*a*) Buenas noches, madrecita.	Good night, mother dear.
(*b*) ¡Qué pintorzuelo!	What a bad artist!
3. (*a*) ¿Cuándo vendrán? Prontito.	When will they come? Very soon.
(*b*) Entró callandito.	He came in quietly.

1 In conversation their use is frequent.

4. (*a*) Me entregó un cucharón.   He handed me a ladle.
   (*b*) Esta mujer es una picaro-   This woman is a rogue.
        naza.
   (*c*) Me dió un codazo.   He gave me a push with his
                                      elbow.
5. (*a*) Es un librote sin valor.   It is a worthless book.
   (*b*) ¿Qué piensa Vd. de aquél   What do you think of that daub?
        mamarracho?
   (*c*) Su cuartucho era sucio.   His wretched room was dirty.

XXVI. *Translate:*

1. What a sweet little-animal (*animalito*)! It is as small as a kitten.
2. A little-voice (*vocecita*) was heard to say 'May I come in?'
3. Offer a seat to that dear-little-old-man (*viejecito*).
4. You are like a ragamuffin (*rapazuelo*)! Go and tidy yourself.
5. We go to bed very early (*tempranito*).
6. I remember it all, every-bit-of-it (*todito*).
7. Would you like a little (*poquito*) more?
8. An enormous-dog (*perrazo*) attacked the children.
9. A huge-man (*hombrón*) was lying on the bed.
10. Did you hear that gunshot (*fusilazo*) on the other side of the
    field?
11. I don't care for that rich-fellow (*ricacho*).
12. That miserable-cottage (*casucha*) ought to be burnt.

§ 77.   MISCELLANEOUS SENTENCES

1. It is good to get up early but pleasanter to stay in bed.
2. A drunken old soldier came to the door.
3. Do you speak Castilian? I speak Spanish, if that's what you mean.
4. The prisoner appeared before the judge.
5. I don't believe in it now and I never shall.
6. How far do you want me to take you?
7. He was a friendless orphan, much to be pitied.
8. I will have the car cleaned by to-morrow.
9. Please ask the servant to take the luggage down.
10. They are to attend the royal inspection in the palace grounds.
11. Mr Charles Francis is very sorry, but he is unable to accept your kind invitation.
12. Bread is sold here at a price higher than we paid in Seville.
13. Reading aloud should be constantly practised.
14. The crops of Canada are enormous.
15. The hat, boots and cloak are lying on the floor.
16. After dinner, in accordance with what had been previously arranged, everyone drove to the theatre.
17. The Tagus and the Seine are two of the rivers I have seen.
18. That artist and the novelist are compatriots.
19. Her ball dress cost more than £10.
20. He was wearing a long sleeveless coat and a broad-brimmed hat.
21. That system is the one I approve of.
22. He fought for their lives and his own.

23. Eighteen hundred fruit trees were uprooted by the storm.
24. The boat sails at eleven to-morrow night.
25. The ditch is deep and is seven feet wide.
26. They came to me without any reason.
27. We English are always grumbling about something.
28. I have bitten my tongue. How it hurts!
29. Almost weeping ourselves, we tried to comfort the weeping women.
30. The hotel was supposed to have running water in all the bedrooms; but it was not running when I was there.
31. Something dark and fairly large was floating on the water.
32. What are the methods he employs to get money from you?
33. His idea is a good one and ought to be put into practice.
34. We passed through beautiful gardens, whose flowers filled the air with scent.
35. Travellers rarely visited the village we were in.
36. I always take as much sugar as I want.
37. May I introduce to you my elder brother?
38. Every hard-working boy benefits from his work.
39. He is the only son of his mother and she is a widow.
40. They were thoroughly ashamed of themselves.
41. My book is with my brother's.
42. Of these two apples this one is ripe, that one unripe.
43. How did your friend come into the building?
44. Is he speaking of them?
45. Whom did his father meet on his way to the station?
46. There is my old master whose enthusiasm always inspired me.
47. This tree is higher than the one in my garden.
48. I will go and look for the man.

49. What you say is the truth.
50. Such a dog and such a strong one too would frighten anyone.
51. I met him a month ago at my sister's.
52. How long have you been working?
53. You are older than I am; I am eighteen.
54. Let us go and sit on the river bank.
55. If they had not gone to Germany and Italy, they would have arrived last Monday.
56. I must lend them to him; he has asked me for them.
57. When you see her you will doubtless speak to her.
58. Joan has just received the flowers from Henry.
59. Give me some or I will take them from you.
60. I am reading the long letter my uncle wrote to me.
61. Do not show them to anyone.
62. I don't remember it; so think no more about it.
63. Miss White sent for Isabel and explained the matter to her.
64. It will be better for you to write now.
65. Who gave it you? No one gave it me.
66. What beautiful weather it is to-day! Yes, isn't it?
67. Don't you remember him? No, I do not.
68. He asked us which road he ought to take.
69. Whose is the beautiful inkstand I see on the table?
70. "Where do you come from?" I asked them.
71. Although I was staying in his house, I never saw him.
72. Do you want me to read you something?
73. I will ask the bookseller at 20 University Street for my book.
74. He is very like his father.
75. What are you thinking about?
76. They were laughing at us the whole time.
77. He may come next month.

78. He knows how to swim, doesn't he?
79. If he comes before one o'clock I will see him, but not otherwise.
80. However rich you are, you should take care not to grow selfish.
81. Sell as quickly as possible whatever jewels you have.
82. Have you ever bathed here? Never.
83. Is he still in Paris? No, he isn't.
84. Have they gone to South America? Yes, they have.
85. Whoever you meet, don't be afraid.
86. Whose pen is this? It looks like mine.
87. A friend of yours will always be a friend of mine.
88. What will become of his young children?
89. He was born at Cadiz on the 21st of June, 1900.
90. Look at this rose. How beautiful it is!
91. What do you think of him and his political views?
92. He went away without my seeing him.
93. Good morning! What sort of weather is it to-day? Is it fine or is it raining?
94. There were more than ten boys in this tiny room.
95. I still don't understand what that lout of a man means.
96. What I am going to tell you, none of your neighbours must know.
97. He who makes my son return home shall have half of my fortune.
98. I was upstairs lying on my bed, overcome by the heat.
99. He didn't know what to do with his son who wouldn't work.
100. He is standing in the water up to his knees.
101. What has become of her since the day before yesterday?
102. Have you nothing better to do than waste your time?
103. My father has asked me if I want to go abroad.

104. Don't sit there; sit here on this comfortable chair.
105. When my brother is ill he doesn't like resting but to go on working.
106. I go to bed at ten; I have breakfast at eight in the morning.
107. How long did you sleep? Seven or eight hours.
108. I am reading the life of Charles the Twelfth by the great Voltaire.
109. He broke his arm playing football.
110. What are you going to do to-day? Tidy my room most of the time.
111. Even if I had any money I wouldn't lend it you.
112. Any day will suit me; only let me know in time.
113. Bring your friend with you, and the dog too.
114. He had hardly spoken when the door opened.
115. Parrots are noisy birds.
116. His house has been empty for six days.
117. I remember it as if it were now.
118. The good is much to be desired.
119. I will stop here until you come.
120. They came in order to see the horses which are for sale.
121. What have I to do with him?
122. What are you complaining of? Stop worrying.
123. They prevented our coming yesterday.
124. I have never seen your curtains. What colour are they?
125. It's colder to-day. I wish it were warmer like the summer days last year.
126. We like holidays; they are never long enough.
127. Open the door and shut the window, please.
128. They raised their hands in horror.
129. What a brave man he is! He fears nothing.
130. Even if we are in Burgos we shall be unable to visit the cathedral.

131. How much are they? Five pesetas each. I will take six of them.
132. He lent me all the books I wanted.
133. We shall have to take something with us.
134. Will you give me a room for to-night? There isn't one.
135. Those who travel learn a great deal.
136. Some of my schoolfellows learnt a foreign language and are now able to earn money by teaching it.
137. Do not fail to write when you get there.
138. I have not seen him for a fortnight.
139. I have been in England longer than you would imagine.
140. We are the ones who saw it.
141. Come again to-morrow; I am at home in the evenings.
142. There has been a good deal of rain this year.
143. As soon as we reached the station the train began to move.
144. On seeing his brother fall he ran to help him.
145. It doesn't matter who comes; there will be no one here.
146. Get up quickly, child, and wash; your father wants you to go with him.
147. Without looking or listening, he jumped from the window.
148. What an extraordinary thing! I have never seen anything like it.
149. However soon he comes, I shall have gone.
150. He obeys his master rather than his parents.
151. I was very wet, but he was not.
152. It gets colder and colder. What will become of us?
153. All, both women and children, perished.
154. You have more than you want.
155. We met them five weeks ago whilst travelling through Switzerland.

156. He allowed himself to be insulted by his friend.
157. When they came I told you what you ought to have said.
158. He is to see me to-morrow morning and you must be there too.
159. I didn't want to read anything.
160. Let us think about our work now.
161. Wherever Mary went her pet lamb was sure to go.
162. Whatever flowers she bought they will die very soon.
163. The more he ate, the better he got.
164. They might have come with us if they had had the time.
165. He made signals to me, now with one hand now with the other.
166. He is one of those people who are too rich to enjoy life.
167. You read and write as well as I do.
168. The Conservatives as well as the Liberals have much to gain in this Election.
169. They don't even offer me a seat.
170. More than 500 books were sold.
171. He thanked me very much for coming.
172. Knock and the door will open; go in and it will shut behind you.
173. Breakfast has been ready for ten minutes.
174. They shivered as if they were cold.
175. Their flags have been hung next to ours.
176. I never play with those who cheat.
177. She wrote to me a few days ago about him.
178. As for you, I can do nothing for you.
179. We heard the children talking in the next room.
180. Travelling for pleasure is often profitable as well.
181. Go straight up the road until you come to the second house on the left.

182. Not only white roses were put on the table, but red also.
183. By dint of much work he succeeded in obtaining what he had wanted for a long time.
184. All his relations were with him except his mother.
185. They were five miles away from one another.
186. I didn't want to go, neither did they.
187. I have worked for many months and need a holiday.
188. What a pity! But there's no help for it; you will have to go.
189. It is to be hoped he will get the boxes sent.
190. They saw him coming in before I had time to stop them.
191. The less he tried, the less, of course, he learnt.
192. When I was your age I loved dancing.
193. When I am older I shall give up running.
194. There is a man in the fourth row who hasn't taken his hat off. Please ask him to do so.
195. The windows are broken, but it is not known by whom.
196. They ate more than they wanted; which was absurd.
197. I have hardly a moment to spare.
198. We had just finished breakfast when the postman appeared.
199. You must have dropped it as you got down from the carriage.
200. I don't worry about other people's affairs.

§ 78.   PROSE SELECTIONS

1

I confess that I am a Galician, from the very centre[1] of Galicia, since I was born in a little town of the province of Orense, called Bollo. My father, an apothecary of this town, has no child save myself, and has built-up[2] for me a fortune which, counting-for[3] little at Madrid, in Bollo almost turned us into potentates! I passed-through[4] the secondary-school-course[5] at Orense, and the faculty of medicine at Santiago. My father would have liked me to be a chemist, but I never had any leaning-towards[6] pounding and evolving drugs. Moreover, in the Institute at Orense I observed that my companions considered medicine as a nobler calling[7], and this made me decide to turn completely away from my father's profession. As soon as I had terminated the course[8], I obtained leave from him, not without some trouble, to take the year's medical course at Madrid, and to-that-place[9] I betook myself, where instead of strengthening my knowledge of the medical sciences which was certainly not very sound, I threw-away[10] a good deal of time in the *cafés*, and, what is worse, contracted a fatal craze[11] for literature.

1 riñon.	2 labrar.	3 significar.	4 cursar.
5 segunda enseñanza.		6 afición a.	7 .ejercicio.
8 carrera.	9 a la Corte.	10 perder.	11 manía.

2

Nemesio told us at-great-length[1] about his country, home, family, character and all-the[2] circumstances which could be directly or indirectly useful for his biography. He was a rich landowner of Simancas, where he had been born and brought up, and he had a wife and seven children, four of them married. The solemn and conscientious exposition which he gave us of the character of each of his sons-in-law and daughters-in-law lasted nearly an hour. The Catalán, when he judged it convenient, made a pillow of his cloak and stretched himself at-full-length on the seat[3]. It was not long before he was snoring[4].

1 prolijamente.   2 cuantas.   3 a lo largo.   4 *tr*.: no tardó en roncar.

3

The train drew up. 'Argamasilla, five minutes stop[1],' shouted someone. I gave a jump in my seat and hastened to open the little window, fixing my eyes eagerly on the darkness of the plain. That name had made my heart give a leap[2]; it was the country of the famous *Don Quixote de la Mancha*; and although as a lyric poet I have always depreciated novelists for their lack of ideal, yet the name of Cervantes fascinated my mind through the great fame which he enjoys throughout the world. Far away the black silhouette of the town was visible, and over it rose a tiny tower, its belfry standing-out[3] clearly against the dark background of the night.

1 de parada.   2 vuelco.   3 destacar.

4

The omnibus lurched[1] over the stones[2], thoroughly[3] shaking us up, sometimes causing our heads to knock-against[4] the roof. Through the small windows we could touch the whitewashed walls of the houses. The landlord of the *Fonda Continental*, a man of medium age and stature, with a large and thick moustache, and dark and gentle eyes, did not take his eyes off[5] us, gazing at us with an attentive

and humble expression, like that of a Newfoundland dog[6].
When at last God willed that the coach should stop, he
jumped lightly to the ground and gallantly offered his hand
to help us to descend. I did not accept through modesty.

| 1 saltar | 2 empedrado. | 3 en todos sentidos. |
| 4 tocar. | 5 apartar. | 6 Terranova. |

5

We stopped in front of a house, as small as all the others;
with one storey, two balconies and two large grated[1]
windows on the level of the ground. The door too had a *reja*,
through which could be seen a patio with tiled[2] pavement
and marble columns where were big flower-pots with flowers
and plants. 'How Moorish[3]!' I exclaimed to myself whilst
I looked everywhere for the knocker. At last I came upon[4]
a little cord; I pulled[5] it and the bell rang.

| 1 enrejadas. | 2 de azulejos. | 3 árabe. |
| 4 dar con. | 5 tirar de. | |

6

The town is very small; it-is-left-behind[1] in a moment.
We went towards the *sierra* which is[2] two or three kilo-
metres off[2]. The *sierra morena* has neither the elevation nor
the elegance, nor the picturesque and graceful brilliance of
the mountains of my country. It is a wild and gloomy region
in which extend for many leagues the dark green ridges,
and where the footstep of man in pursuit of deer or wild
boar comes but rarely. Nevertheless the contrast of that
dark curtain of hills with the dove-like-whiteness[3] of the
town makes it pleasing to the eyes and poetical. By a gentle
slope, along a track made for-the-purpose[4], we descended
to the stream which gushes[5] from the very centre of the

Guadalquivir, which engirdles[6] the skirt of the *sierra*. There is a passage-way[7] or bridge which leads from the bank to the spring. Along it were gravely strolling two or three dozen people, revealing by their vague and distracted looks that they were paying more attention to what was going on in the interior of their bodies than to the conversation or passage of their companions. Now and then they darted[8] to the spring, descended the small ladders, asked for a glass of water and drank-it-off[9] greedily.

1 se sale de él.	2 distar.	3 blancura de paloma.
4 al intento.	5 salir.	6 venir ciñendo.
7 galería.	8 se dirigían con pie rápido.	9 beberse.

7

The engine was steaming[1] through the fields of the Province of Cordoba. Covered with budding[2] corn they stretched out in a plain of pale green, terminating abruptly at the dark and uncultivated wall of the *sierra*. As we drew near to the city, I was vividly impressed by the memories evoked by its grandeur. That mass[3] of houses which stood up[4] grey and melancholy between the river and the mountain had been the great city of the West, the capital of the civilised world. Years and years, centuries and centuries of silence and sadness had succeeded the noise and cheerfulness which doubtless reigned[5] there formerly. In my imagination I saw it beautiful and happy in the midst of a fruitful smiling district, abounding in every kind of harvest[6], occupying a huge area[7] with its shining ramparts furnished with monumental gates, and innumerable streets where watering-machines[8] laid[9] the dust. Travellers without number passed through these streets going in and out of the bazaars at whose doors hung rich damasks and tapestries. In every direction[10] rose sumptuous palaces; in many places were

planted groves and public gardens where happy loungers[11]
inhaled the scent of orange-blossom and cinnamon. Erect[12]
over the minaret of the mosque the crescent raised its
powerful horns protecting the city.

1 correr.   2 tiernos.   3 montón.   4 alzarse.
5 *imp. subj. (for conditional).*   6 cosechas.   7 extensión.
8 máquinas de riego. 9 abatir.   10 en todas partes. 11 moradores.
12 enhiesta.

8

We were approaching Seville! I felt my heart beating
strongly. Seville had always been for me the symbol of light,
the city of love and happiness. Orchards of orange trees
could now be seen, and among their emerald[1] branches
like ruby globes—as-an-Arab-poet-puts-it[2]—peeped out the
oranges which were melting away, so-ripe-were-they[3]. In
the neighbouring[4] stations I noticed on the platforms a
certain animation, which could not have been caused by us
passengers. Black-eyed girls, with red carnations in their
hair, standing[5] on the platform smiled at those of-us[6] who
appeared[7] at the windows. All the signalmen's-little-houses[8]
had flower boxes in their windows. Even the *guardesas*, old
and poorly clad, who with flag furled[9] let[10] the train go by,
boasted[11] in their grey hair some carnation or gilliflower[12].
Right on the horizon I saw a high tower and at the side of it
various others of smaller dimensions. 'Seville, Seville,' I cried,
unable to repress the extraordinary and lively emotion which
was dominating me.

1 de esmeralda.   2 según la expresión de un poeta arábigo.
3 de puro maduras.   4 prójimas.   5 de pie.   6 *omit.*
7 asomarse.   8 casetas de guardas.   9 recogida.
10 dar paso.   11 ostentar.   12 alelí.

9

I was in the chapel but I could see scarcely any[1] of it, such was the darkness which prevailed[2]. I could see, however, that it was fairly large and well appointed[3]. The high altar and everything around it stood-out[4] clearly owing to the light which fell from the little windows of the dome; but from that-part[5] to the back where I was standing, the shadows grew-gradually-thicker[6]. I stood[7] undecided till the nun, striking[8] a match, pointed out to me some *reclinatorios* of red velvet which were placed-against[9] the back wall. I took[10] the nearest one, but she compelled me to move along[11] to the furthest, without doubt so that those who came afterwards should find no difficulty in-passing[12]. She then withdrew wishing me good-day, and going up to a rope which was hanging from the roof she began to pull it vigorously.

1 nada.	2 reinar.	3 decorada.	4 designarse.
5 allí.	6 irse espesando.	7 permanecer.	8 *tr. by* sacar.
9 arrimado.	10 acomodarme.	11 correrse.	12 al pasar.

10

At-that-time[1] there occurred in the house where I was living an unhappy incident which, although it did not touch me closely[2], did not fail to impress me. One morning, a little before lunch, I noticed a certain activity (going on). Matildita was fluttering about like a frightened linnet: the servants were coming and going with little bottles and flasks in[3] their hands. I asked what was happening, and they told me that[4] the *señora* had fallen[5] suddenly ill—'a heart attack,' they said. 'She was so stout!' I went to her room and they told me the doctor was inside. I waited a moment and saw him leave with Torres who was extremely pale. The doctor also wore an anxious look. Poor Torres was[6] so preoccupied that he did not even notice[7] me. I had to attract his attention. He sat down on the sofa and in a trembling voice and with a frightened air told me how it happened.

| 1 por aquellos días. | 2 de cerca. | 3 entre. | 4 de que. |
| 5 ponerse. | 6 andar. | 7 reparar en. | |

11

The exquisite prose-writer describes to us in his work the type of a radical politician, a revolutionary, sprung[1] from the womb of the people, one who has attained to an eminent position. He has everything: prestige, eloquence, strength of will, wealth, innumerable and enthusiastic adherents[2]. All this he has won; all is the result of his perseverance and his indomitable will-power[3]. By what means has he attained to his dizzy[4] position? Let us not speak of this; it is to be feared, by all the means open to him. He only lacks one thing: the sanction of that part of society—the aristocratic, the intellectual—into which he was not born. This is a profoundly interesting psychological trait[5]; these men of the people, helped-upwards[6] by fortune, do not consider themselves completely happy in their prosperity, if they do not possess that-very-thing[7] against which they have directed their attacks.

| 1 salido. | 2 parciales. | 3 querer. | 4 encumbrada. |
| 5 rasgo. | 6 aupado. | 7 aquello mismo. | |

12

To organise, to construct, to weave an extensive and dense warp[1] of partisans[2] and associations through the whole of Spain; when has this been achieved in our midst[3]? Do-we-picture-ourselves[4] like those great, strong, tireless North American politicians who in the lapse of one day, dashing along giddily in a special train, pronounce eight, fifteen speeches before as-many[5] crowds and leave a deep impression[6] of cordiality and confidence in thousands and thousands of hearts? No, here is the Spanish type: a parliamentarian, ensconced[7] in his office, inaccessible to the coreligionist[8], to the friend, to the admirer, holding his reception[9] at a fixed hour, taking a stroll at another fixed hour, preparing a 'great speech[10]' for a week, answering a friendly letter with vague and diffuse *formulae*, expanding into theatrical gestures and emphatic phrases. Everything is rigid, without spontaneity or effusion, without warmth, without enthusiasm, without life. Everything (is) lifeless in a lifeless country.

1 urdimbre.	2 partidarios.	3 entre nosotros.	4 imaginarse.
5 otras tantas.	6 rastro.	7 metido.	8 correligionario.
9 tertulia.	10 'gran discurso.'		

13

A spider of enormous size, a huge body squatting[1] on eight furry legs, was climbing rapidly up the wall, trying to escape the light. Its progress was so rapid, that the *señorito* tried without success to reach it with his boot. Suddenly Nucha stepped forward and in a voice half serious, half frightened, exclaimed ingenuously what she had said a thousand times in her childhood: 'St George[2], spiders[3]!' The ugly insect stopped at the edge of the shadow; the boot fell on it. Julian, through a natural reaction from that kind of fear which dissipated changes into inexplicable delight, was-about-to[4] laugh at[5] the incident, but he noticed that Nucha, closing her eyes and leaning against the wall, was covering her face with her handkerchief. 'It is nothing, it is nothing,' she murmured.

1 columpiar.	2 San Jorge.	3 para la araña.	4 ir a.	5 de.

14

At that moment a man of sinister appearance, hidden up to then in a corner, appeared at-the-side-of¹ the attorney's table. He was dressed not as a labourer but like a low-conditioned² person of the town; he wore a jacket of black cloth, a red sash and a grey slouch hat; short whiskers with a hatchet-shaped jaw³ redoubled the hardness of his face with its salient⁴ cheekbones and wide temples. The lawyer, opening the drawer of his desk, drew from it two huge horse-pistols⁵, and examined them, to make-sure⁶ that they were loaded. Looking at the newcomer⁷ fixedly, he appeared to offer them to him with a slight raising of the eyebrows. For-sole⁸ reply the other pointed to the handle of a knife protruding from his belt.

1 junto a.	2 de baja condición.	3 boca de hacha.
4 abultados.	5 pistolas de arzón.	6 cerciorarse.
7 aparecido.	8 por toda.	

15

The cross now loomed-dark¹ above them, and Julian began to recite in a very low tone the accustomed *paternoster*. He was walking in front, and the *señorito* was almost treading-on² his heels. The baggage boys had-gone-on³ a long way ahead, as-they-wished-to⁴ arrive as soon as possible at the village and to have a drink at the inn. The senses of a huntsman were in truth needed to hear the whispering noise which the leaves and thicket produced as they parted to make-passage⁵ for a human body. The *señorito* heard it and saw the rifle barrel pointing not at his breast but at Julian's back. D. Pedro was almost paralysed by surprise: it was a second, less than a second perhaps, an inappreciable interval of time which he needed to recover himself and to raise[6] his weapon, aiming in his turn at the ambushed enemy.

| 1 negrear. | 2 pisar. | 3 adelantarse. |
| 4 deseosos de. | 5 abrir paso. | 6 echarse a la cara. |

16

No one took any notice of her cries of consternation; but after a few minutes had-passed[1], the judge in person appeared in the hall. He overwhelmed himself in excuses for the stupidity[2] of the servant girl; 'It was inconceivable the trouble it cost to train[3] them; you repeated to them the same thing a thousand times and it-was-no-good[4]....' Murmuring on in this way, he crooked[5] his elbow, offering the lady the support of his arm to climb the staircase, which was so narrow that there-was-not-room[6] for two persons abreast. Having arrived at the drawing-room door the judge began to feel about, anxiously looking for something in his pockets. Suddenly he gave vent to a kind of terrible roar. 'Pepa, the key, where have you put the key?' Pepa dashed off at-full-speed[7] and the judge changing his tone of hoarse fury to one of mellifluous gentleness pushed open the door and said, 'This-way[8], madam, please.' The room was in-complete-darkness[9]. The lady stumbled-up-against[10] a table whilst the judge kept on saying, 'Please sit down, madam; forgive me.'

1 transcurridos.	2 torpeza.	3 domesticar.	4 nada.
5 arquear.	6 caber.	7 a toda prisa.	8 por aquí.
9 completamente a obscuras.		10 tropezar con.	

17

Plutarch's[1] work[2] has been compared with a full-flowing[3] stream, which flows noiselessly and without effort through an extensive countryside, which it irrigates and fertilises

with its waters. The plan of his work is probably unique
of its kind. From-the-outset[4] the two most celebrated
nations of antiquity, the one for her arts and genius[5], the
other for her strength and grandeur, are seen competing in
talent, virtue and glory. Then the reader's gaze is fastened
on the portraits of great men which that vast gallery
contains, each of whom makes a deep impression on his
nation. This man gives laws, that man customs; one protects
her from invasion, another carries-her-off[6] to conquest; this
one wishes to save her from the corruption with which she
is infected, that one kindles the torch which is destined to
purify her; all possessing characters peculiarly adapted[7]
either to virtue and talent, or to vice and crime; and almost
all suffering a violent death because the reforms and reactions
which-they-brought-about[8] in others produced at last that
insanity which devoured themselves.

1 Plutarco.   2 obra.   3 caudaloso.   4 desde luego.
5 ingenio.   6 arrebatar.   7 dispuestos.   8 de que son causa.

18

And what nation is there which has not its heroes to be
admired and imitated? What nation is there which has not
suffered vicissitudes from good[1] to evil and from evil to good,
since the time when these extraordinary men have been
created? It will certainly not be that nation which in the
northern mountains of Spain raised the standard of inde-
pendence against the fanatical onset of the Arabs. There
it not only maintained itself[2] free from the oppression
under which the rest of the Peninsula was groaning, but
acquiring force and daring, descended to drive its foes from
the wide territory where they were (settled). Without as-
sistance, without the support of any foreign prince or nation,

divided against itself either by the partition of states un-
wisely established by their kings, or through the civil wars
which these states waged on one another; having to confront
at the same time fresh floods of barbarians which Africa sent
from time to time as reinforcements; it nevertheless for
seven whole centuries struggled on, in a terrible series of
combats, perils and victories. At length the Mussulman left
Spain and then as a smothered fire breaks out and extends
far and wide, so the Spaniard became lord-over[3] half of
Europe, throwing the whole continent into agitation with
his ambitious activity, spreading himself over vast unknown
oceans, giving a new world to mankind.

1 bien.   2 *historic present to the end of the piece.*   3 enseñorearse.

19

The waters of Malta were the scene of Roger's first victory.
He-had-been-warned[1] that the French galleys were sailing
round that island to succour the fortress which was being
besieged by the Aragonese, and straightway he left with his
own ships to encounter the French. He found them unpre-
pared[2] in the harbour, and although he could have attacked
them unexpectedly, he preferred to wait for day, and sent
them a skiff to order them to surrender or to get ready for
battle. The enemy's galleys numbered twenty, and his own
eighteen; at daybreak there-was-a-general-engagement[3], and
they fought with as much tenacity and fury as if the resto-
ration of Sicily depended on that day. Half the day was
gone, and the action was still going on, when the French
commander saw that his galleys were giving-way[4] and on
the point of fleeing. His name was Guillaume Carner and
he was endowed with extraordinary valour; kindled into

fury at the weakness of his men, he determined to-stake-everything-on-one-throw[5], and with great boldness attacked Roger's vessel, thinking victory would be his if[6] it were taken or destroyed. He boarded it by the prow; with a battle-axe[7] he cut-his-way[8] through the midst of his foes striking them down and slaying them. Roger rushed to meet him and the two fought one-another[9] with the strength for which they were noted and with the fury which animated them. A spear transfixed[10] Roger by the foot to the deck whilst a stone struck[11] Guillaume's axe from his hand. Then the Spanish general, who had been able to wrench-out[12] the spear, flung it at his adversary who fell lifeless to the deck.

1 tener aviso.   2 descuidades.   3 embestir unas con otras.
4 ceder.   5 aventurar todo de una vez.
6 en *with infin.*   7 hacha de armas.   8 hacerse camino.   9 entre sí.
10 clavar.   11 derribar.   12 desclavarse.

20

The news of this conspiracy reached him at the time when he was at the arsenal hurrying-on[1] the preparations for the expedition; and just as he was, covered with dust, ill-clad, and girt only with a towel, he rushed indignantly to the palace, and, brought before[2] the king and those vile courtiers, he said: 'Which of you knowing nothing of my hardships, is not satisfied with what I have done up to the present? I am here, let him voice his accusation and I will reply to him. If you depreciate[3] my actions and my labours, by means of which you hold your lives and your wealth, show what you have done and whether your victories have won the home[4] and Fatherland in which you live, the luxury which you display. You amused yourselves whilst I was op-pressed by weight of arms; no anxiety agitated you whilst

I was settling my campaigns; you were idle; I feared neither death nor fatigue; I was exposed to the inclemency of the sea; you were sheltered in your houses. An oarsman's bench was my couch, and my dishes were repugnant to you, accustomed as you are to dainty[5] tables; in fine, hunger and anxiety consumed me whilst you, given up to pleasure, found your safety in my labours. Think on my actions and consider, if the war lasts, who is to be the scourge of your enemies. Your calumny does not shame me as much as your peril grieves me, should you forget what I am worth and should you cast me away[6] from you.'

1 dar prisa á.	2 puesto delante.	3 *2nd plural to the end.*
4 hogar.	5 regalado.	6 desechar.

21

At daybreak on the following day, the 2nd June 1453, he heard mass, devoutly received-the-Communion[1], and prepared to go to the place of execution. He asked that something should be given him to drink, and they brought him a dish of berries[2], of which he ate a few, and then drank a cup of wine. He then mounted a mule and they drew him through the streets to the *Plaza Mayor*, where the scaffold was raised, the crier[3] proclaiming the sentence, which he carried before him in a cleft[4] reed. 'This is the sentence which our lord the King orders to-be-carried-out[5] on this cruel tyrant, usurper of the royal crown.' When he came to the scaffold they made him dismount, and he ascended the steps briskly and with firm resolution. By chance his eyes fell on one of the two pages who had attended him in prison, and giving him a ring and his hat, he said, 'Take this gift, the last you can receive from me.' The boy lifted up his voice in doleful weeping, which was echoed by the spectators, who

had up to then kept a profound silence. The priests[6] urged
him not to meditate on his former greatness but to think
only of dying like a good Christian. 'That-I-do[7],' he replied,
'and rest assured that I die with the same faith as the
martyrs.'

1 comulgar.   2 guindas.   3 pregonero.   4 hendida.
5 hacer.   6 religiosos.   7 así lo hago.

22

Luna enjoyed his life in the army with-its-freedom-and-
lawlessness[1], like a schoolboy who leaves his confinement,
but he could not conceal from himself the painful disil-
lusionment[2] which the sight of those armies of the Faith
produced in him. He had thought to find something similar
to the old expeditions of the Crusades: soldiers who fought
for an ideal, who bent the knee before going into battle so
that God should be with them, and who at night, after
fierce combats, slept the pure sleep of the ascetic. But
actually he found armed flocks disobedient to their shepherd,
incapable of the fanaticism which runs blindly to death,
only desirous that[3] the war should go on as long as possible,
so as to maintain at the country's cost their vagrant and
slothful life, which was in their opinion the most perfect
form of existence.

1 tr.: *free and without laws.*   2 decepción.   3 ganosos de que.

23

For a long time the two men strolled along in silence.
But Antolín could not easily remain silent when the-con-
versation-turned-on[1] the economic life of the mother-church.
'To think, Gabriel,' he continued, 'that being what we have
been in other times, we-should-be-brought-to-such-a-pass[2]!

You and the majority of those who live here have no idea
how-rich[3] this place has been. It has been as wealthy as a
king and sometimes even wealthier. As[4] a boy you knew
better-than-anyone[5] the history of our glorious archbishops,
but you knew nothing of the fortunes they amassed for the
glory of God, nothing at all[6]! You scholars are-not-con-
cerned-with[7] "materialistic"-considerations[8]. Do you know
of the gifts which kings and nobles in their lifetime made
to this cathedral and the legacies which they bequeathed in
the hour of their death? How-should-you-know[9]? But I
know all about it. Let each man study what interests him
most, and I, who have raged[10] more than once at the poverty
of the building, console myself thinking of what it had
before we were born.'

1 tratarse de.	2 nos vemos así.	3 lo rica que.	4 de.
5 como nadie.	6 ni una palabra.	7 darse por.	
8 materialidades.	9 ¿Qué has de conocer?	10 rabiar.	

24

The cathedral had dominion over land, sea and air. Our
authority extended over the whole country, from-end-to-
end[1]; there was not a province where we did not possess
something. Everything contributed to the glory of God and
to the propriety[2] and well-being of his ministers; everything
paid its share to the cathedral: The bread baking[3] in the
oven; the fish falling[3] into the net, the corn passing[3] through
the mill, the money coming[3] from the die[4], the traveller
pursuing[3] his journey. The peasants, who at that time did
not pay contribution or taxes[5], served their king and saved
their own souls giving us the best sheaf[6] from every ten, so
that the granaries of the mother church were not large
enough to hold such opulence[7]. What times those were!

There was faith then, and faith is the-main-thing[8] in life.
Without faith there is no virtue, no propriety,...nothing!

1 de punta a punta. 2 decencia. 3 al *with infin.* 4 troquel.
5 impuestos. 6 gavilla. 7 abundancia. 8 lo principal.

25

How I envy you, you who have travelled and have heard
such fine things! The other night I couldn't sleep thinking
of what you told me of your life in Paris; those delightful
Sunday afternoons hastening after lunch, sometimes to the
Concerts Lamoureux, at other times to the *Concerts Colonne,*
regaling yourself with a surfeit of sublimity! And, I, shut
up here, without-hope-of-doing-anything-save[1] conducting
some wretched-little-mass[2] of Rossini at the great festivals!
My sole consolation is to read music, to learn through
reading the great works which so many dozing[3] bored
imbeciles will hear in the towns. I have here in this heap
the nine symphonies of the Man, his many sonatas, his Mass.
I have too Haydn, Mozart, Mendelssohn, in a word, all the
great ones[4]. I even have Wagner. I read them. I play what
I can, and-all-for-what[5]? It is as if you described eloquently
to a blind man the design of a picture and its colours. Buried
in this cloister of Toledo, I know, as the blind man knows,
that there are in the world very lovely things...but, like him,
only-through-hearsay[6].

1 sin otra esperanza que. 2 misita. 3 dormitar.
4 tíos. 5 ¿y qué? 6 de oídas.

26

He stopped and, looking all around, seemed impatient and
uneasy. Without doubt he had no great confidence in the
accuracy of his direction and was waiting for some villager

to pass by to give him correct information for arriving speedily and by-the-most-direct-way[1] at his destination. 'I cannot be mistaken,' he murmured, 'they told me to cross the river by the stepping-stone[2]. I did so. Then they told me to go straight-on[3]. I like that phrase "straight on," and, if I had a coat-of-arms[4], I would not place any other motto[5] on it. "Straight on," and I am to arrive at the mines. I seem to be in a desert. What solitude! If I believed in witches, I would think that my fate was preparing for me the honour of being introduced to them. Heavens, are there no people hereabouts? It still wants half an hour till the moon rises. Ah, wretch, you are-to-blame[6] for my losing my way.' He took a step forward and sank into the shifting[7] ground. 'So-that's-it[8], Mr Planet? You want to swallow me up? What's this? A stone: magnificent seat to smoke a cigar on, waiting for the moon to rise!'

| 1 derechamente. | 2 pasadera. | 3 adelante. | 4 escudo. |
| 5 divisa. | 6 tener la culpa. | 7 movediza. | 8 ¡esas tenemos! |

27

'Your blind master loves you very much?' Yes, sir, he is very kind. He says that he sees with my eyes, because I take him everywhere and tell him how everything looks. He asks me what[1] a star is like, and I describe it for him in such a way that for him it is the same as though he saw it. I explain to him the grasses, the clouds, the sky, the water, lightning, moths, butterflies, smoke, shells, the bodies and faces of persons and animals. I tell him what is ugly and what is beautiful, and so he-gradually-learns-about[2] everything.

| 1 como. | 2 irse enterando de. |

28

A peasant, who takes delight in farthings[1] and dreams of[2] changing them into silver to convert the silver afterwards into gold, is the most ignoble animal that can be-imagined[3]; he has all the tricks and subtleties of man and a barrenness[4] of feelings fearful-to-think-upon[5]. His soul gets slowly compressed until it is no more than a calculator[6] of quantities. Ignorance, rusticity, and miserable living complete the portrait of this abominable specimen[7]. Counting on his fingers, he is capable of reducing to figures his conscience, his soul, and the whole of morality.

| 1 ochavos. | 2 con. | 3 imaginarse. | 4 sequedad. |
| 5 que espante. | | 6 graduador. | 7 pieza. |

29

D. Francisco, the young man's father, was extremely tactful[1], kindly, affable, honourable and generous, and not lacking-in[2] culture. No one disliked him; he was the most respected of all the rich landowners of the country, and more than one question was settled by his consistently[3] skilful mediation. The house where we have seen him living was his cradle. He had been to America when[4] a young man, and on returning to Spain without a fortune took service in the national-police[5]. Having retired to his native town, where he gave himself up to farming and cattle-raising[6], he inherited a well-ordered[7] estate, and at the time of our stay had just acquired another. His wife, an Andalusian, had died at a very early age, leaving one son, who, shortly after birth, was found to be completely deprived of the most precious of the senses. This was the most poignant[8] sorrow to the good father and it embittered his life. What mattered it to

H S   6

him to amass wealth and to see fortune favouring his business
and smiling in his home? For whom was it? For one who
could not see the sleek[9] cows or the smiling meadows or the
orchard laden with fruit. D. Francisco would have given his
own eyes to his son, remaining blind for the rest of his life,
if this kind of generosity had been possible in the world as
we know it. But as it is not, he could not give reality to the
noble sentiment of his heart.

1 discreto.	2 falto de.	3 siempre.
4 de.	5 guardia civil.	6 ganadería.
7 regular.	8 aguda.	9 gordas.

30

You have[1] wanted to make me believe that the sun is still
and that the earth moves round it? How can you know what
you do not see? May I die at this moment, if the earth is
not firmer than a rock and the sun is not moving! Do-not-
show-off-your-cleverness[2] so much, my dear master. I have
spent many hours, day and night, looking at the sky. The
sun rises over-there[3] and sets on-the-opposite-side[3] of the
sky. Why should it not be so? Have you noticed the sky
on a clear day? It seems to rain blessings. I don't think
there can be any wicked people; no, there cannot be if they
turn their faces upwards. Think-as-you-will[4]. I have evolved
in my head many things which console me, and so, when a
good idea occurs to me, I say: 'It must be so and not otherwise.' At night, I meditate-on[5] what will become of us when
we die, and on how-much[6] the Holy Virgin loves us.

1 2nd sing. throughout.	2 echárselas de sabio.	3 por allá...por allí.
4 piensa que pensarás.	5 ir pensando en.	6 lo mucho que.

31

I then tried to understand the teacher's explanations. And that was not easy! That good lady had the gift of making the clearest things obscure! I think that no one, not even the best and most progressive[1] members of the course, understood a single word. However, when she asked 'Have you understood?,' everyone answered-in-a-loud-voice[2] 'Yes, miss.' We said this to flatter her, to make a noise, and above all to stop her talking. Her voice was harsh, level and monotonous, and she talked and talked like a phonograph. She had a vocal chord[3] that lasted all day,...all her life in fact. And, in addition, she had eyes at the four corners of her head, because she saw absolutely everything. Not a pin could drop without her seeing it. She enjoyed military discipline, possibly because only thus could she get any at all. With her lungs as strong as those of a horse, she vociferated abuse without ever getting husky or tired. I would begin[4] to draw with chalk on the bench and she would[4] correct me with 'John, don't dirty the form.' I would hunt a[4] fly...'John, don't hunt flies.' I would speak[4] to my neighbour in an undertone...'John, hold your tongue.' And this lasted[4] all through the class.

1 aprovechados.   2 a voz en cuello.   3 cuerda.   4 *imperfect indic.*

32

The fact that it was absolutely impossible for the young subaltern and his *fiancée* to get married, had caused them to hide their affections from others in order not to see them combated. They counted-on[1] time which does so much to smooth out difficulties; they counted on their own constancy to surmount these difficulties, and on their hopes of living,

in the meantime, tranquil and contented. The young man
used to attend[2] the receptions of the marchioness in-the-
ordinary-way[3], without their conversation ever going further
than this, 'My-humble-respects,-dear-lady[4].' 'How are you,
Bruno; very glad to see you.' As for Alegría, this merry
child had not yet surrendered her heart which she guarded
as a sultan does his kerchief, still in-doubt-as-to[5] whom she
would favour with it. Meanwhile, she accepted worship as a
tribute due to her, without[6] this blinding her vision or pre-
venting her from discriminating between the suitors who
were offered her.

1 contar con.	2 asistir a.	3 como uno de tantos.
4 tía, a los pies de Vd.	5 tr.: *doubting*.	6 sin que *with subj.*

33

'What's-the-matter[1] now?' said Doña Eufrasia as she
came in.

'The matter indeed! It is that spendthrift[2] son of mine,
who sends me from Paris a letter-of-exchange[3] for 30,000
reales.'

'It's-your-fault[4]. Why do you pay his debts? The more
you pay, the more he will spend. Squandering is like the
thirst of hypocrisy. The more one drinks, the thirstier one
is.'

'My daughters,' continued the other, 'are the worst
brought up, the most intractable[5], the most disobedient—'

'Your fault[4], because you don't know how to keep discipline in your house.'

'Take Constance, who is the most ungovernable[6] and un-
tamed—'

'On bread and water, rebels become smoother than gloves.'

'My dear[7], she-is-nineteen[8]!'

'Bread and water suit every age,' replied the fierce old lady.

'Then,' continued her friend, 'there is Juanita, who thinks of nothing but amusing herself; the whole day she has been-plaguing[9] me to take her out for a walk. Think of me, walking[10]!'

'Don't give in. Little girls should be seen-and-not-heard[11].'

1 *use* tener.   2 derrochador.   3 letra.   4 tener la culpa.
5 indocil.   6 discola.   7 mujer.
8 *use conditional clause with* si.   9 moler.
10 ¡Para paseos estaba yo!   11 recogidas.

34

'I shall be glad if you will allow me to go to bed at once,' said old[1] Lucas, yawning atrociously. 'Last night I had a lot of milling[2] (to do), and I never closed[3] my eyes.'

'Granted,' replied the *alcalde* pompously. 'You may retire when you like.'

'I think it is time we all retired,' said the sacristan peeping-into[4] the wine bottle to-gauge[5] what was left. 'It must be ten o'clock—or nearly.'

'A quarter to ten,' announced the secretary, after having distributed into the glasses what-was-left[6] of the wine.

'Well, to bed[7], gentlemen!' exclaimed the host, draining his share.

'Till to-morrow, sirs,' added the miller, drinking-off[8] his.

'Wait for a light. Tonuelo! Conduct friend[9] Lucas to the loft.'

'This way,' said Tonuelo, carrying off the bottle as well, on-the-chance-of[10] some drops remaining.

'Till to-morrow, if God wills,' added the sacristan, after draining all the glasses. And he went off, staggering and intoning merrily the *De Profundis*.

1 el tío.   2 molienda.   3 pegar.   4 asomarse a.   5 graduar.
6 el resto. 7 a dormir.   8 beberse.   9 tío.   10 per si.

35

The poor humpback[1] began[2] to cry. Then, to recover himself, he stopped the donkey; dried his tears; sighed deeply; drew out his smoking-apparatus[3]; pricked[4] and rolled[5] a cigar of black tobacco; grasped flint, tinder and steel; and after a few blows succeeded in kindling a light. At that moment he heard a noise of steps in the direction of the road—about 300 yards[6] distant. 'How imprudent of me,' he said. 'If the police[7] were looking for me, I should have given-myself-away[8], lighting that tinder.' He concealed, therefore, the light, and dismounting, hid behind the donkey, who, however, seeing things in-a-different-light[9], emitted a bray of satisfaction. 'A curse-on-you[10],' exclaimed her master, trying to stop her mouth with his hands. At the same instant an answering bray sounded from the road. Immediately he mounted again, spurred-on[11] his beast, and dashed off in the opposite direction. The curious thing was that the person on the second donkey must have been just as frightened of Lucas as Lucas had been of him, because he, too, withdrew from the road, suspecting no doubt that it was[12] a policeman.

1 jorobado.   2 echarse a.   3 avíos de fumar.
4 picar.   5 liar.   6 *use conditional*.
7 la Justicia.   8 venderse.   9 de diferente modo.
10 maldita seas.   11 arrear.   12 *subjunctive*.

36

'My town,' I once heard an opulent country-squire[1] say, 'has changed in a prodigious manner during the war. Its population has doubled; it has built a large market; it has brought drinking water to the public squares and to private dwellings; it has installed electricity, and has built a casino. Soon[2], it will have a magnificent theatre, three cinemas and as-many[3] variety-houses[4].'

'Very good,' I replied. 'I suppose that you have also opened a public library?'

My interlocutor was-dumb[5]. After a long interval of meditation, he put[6] me the following question:

'How is a library formed?'

'By buying books,' I replied immediately.

'What books?' insisted the squire frowning.

'Good heavens[7]! Good books.'

'But what are good books?'

At first I was scandalised at the question; but then I reflected and was[8] perplexed. Which are the most suitable books which ought to be acquired for a popular library?

1 ricacho.	2 dentro de poco.	3 otros tantos.
4 salones de variadades.	5 enmudecerse.	6 hacer.
7 diantre.	8 quedarse.	

37

Other nations, proud of their glories, found museums to preserve in a dignified way what has remained as a memory of their celebrated citizens. France keeps in its entirety the house of Victor Hugo, and very many objects which belonged to Balzac and others; Italy preserves Dante's home exactly as it was when he inhabited it; England has made a sanctuary of Shakespeare's and Germany of Beethoven's. Spain, who boasts so many literary and artistic men as her heritage, does not even watch over the remains of Lope and Cervantes. A country priest[1] threw those of Lope into the charnel-house[2] to bury a sister of his in their place; those of the author of *Quijote* are lost! And nevertheless, many of these relics perchance exist in private houses, through their having been bequeathed from generation to generation. Why does our Government not employ some money in founding, if not a museum, at least a room in any one of them in which could be collected all the relics that could be found of our literary and artistic splendours, which remain the most precious heritage of the Spanish nation?

1 de misa y olla.   2 osario.

38

On-the-occasion-of[1] the festival of Agriculture which takes place every year, coinciding with St Isidor's[2] day, the minister of Agriculture[3] made-a-speech[4] in which, after outlining[5] his programme, he added that the Government would duly support all proposals made on behalf of the industries and progress of the nation. According to him millions of pesetas can be easily found in spite of the economic condition of Spain, which was-shown-clearly-enough[6] in Parliament yesterday to be very unsound. Spain apparently has the capacity to concede the money, the total absence of any financial scheme constituting[7] no insuperable obstacle! When fancy is allowed to govern in this fashion it is not extraordinary that the sad realities of the moment should be forgotten[8]. A few days ago an important meeting took place in Valencia at which the Agriculturists applied to the Government asking that the tax on alcohol should be suppressed[9], that wines should be declared[9] free from all municipal taxation, that special fixed railway tariffs should be reintroduced[9], that the prosecution of fraud[10] should be made[9] effective, and that wine-growing should have in the tariff-department[11] the representation due to it. What will be the reply of the Government to such proposals?

1 con motivo de. 2 Isidro. 3 Fomento.
4 pronunciar un discurso. 5 exponer.
6 ponerse de relieve. 7 sin que *with subjunctive*.
8 *subjunctive*. 9 *subjunctive*. 10 *plural*.
11 Junta de Aranceles.

39

After lunch the King went to the central-hall[1] of the Casino in which the chess tables had been set up. One had been specially arranged so that the King might play with D. Manuel Galmayo, an-officer-of-the-General-Staff[2]. The match[3] began in-an-atmosphere-of[4] great expectancy. It lasted three quarters of an hour and his Majesty won, showing himself to be a formidable exponent of the game, being-a-quick-attacker-and-sure-mover[5]. The King's skill was warmly applauded. On taking his leave he stated[6] to the-chairman-of-the-executive-committee[7] that he had spent a very pleasant afternoon of which he would always retain a grateful remembrance. The Casino of Madrid, the leading club in Spain for its appointments[8] and its methodical and fully democratic administration, may also rest satisfied with yesterday's celebration.

1 salon de actos. 2 comandante de Estado Major. 3 partida.
4 en medio de. 5 tr.: *of quick attack and sure stroke* (golpe).
6 manifestar. 7 presidente de la junta directiva. 8 instalaciones.

40

It seems that aviation in the public service is entering the field[1] of the practical. The progress of the industry is very rapid. Not long ago a journey in an aeroplane was not only rash but vexatious and uncomfortable. At the present time according to the 'Times' all difficulties have-been-sur-mounted[2]. A type of plane has been constructed in which the passenger is able to read, write, converse, eat and sleep. There are small square tables with wicker chairs, a bed with air-mattresses[3], and dividing[4] curtains of silk; and the traveller will find all the conveniences of the trains and steamers of the great maritime and land routes. What the 'Times' does not say is what a kilometric ticket will cost in these new aerial transports.

1 campo.   2 salvarse.   3 colchonetas de aire.   4 aisladoras.

41

When I learnt that Ibáñez was in Madrid, on-his-way-to[1] Valencia, I-felt-I-would-like[2] to go and greet him and hear his warm, vibrant speech, full of brilliance and colour, like the descriptive pictures that his magical pen-brush[3] has painted. Accordingly I wrote to the great Valencian novelist, but telling him that I wanted to visit him at an hour when he was free from reporters, photographers, *tertulianos*, fellow-writers[4], idle admirers, and the whole chorus and customary retinue of those who have won celebrity. I very much wanted to monopolise Blasco Ibáñez for a long chat, during which we should be free from interrupters. And so it turned out. After an effusive and cordial letter, assigning me an hour early-in-the-evening[5], I went to the Palace Hotel, whose bustle and flow[6] of people and resemblance to a huge Atlantic liner, on account of its long rooms and low ceilings, seem to evoke the pages of one of his novels, *The Argonauts*[7]. When at the entrance I asked for Señor Blasco Ibáñez the porter made a gesture[8] of fatigue and resignation. I was without doubt the twentieth person who was asking for the celebrated writer that day. He told me the number; I ascended to the second floor, and in the corridor, looking out through the half-opened door as if he were awaiting me with impatience, I saw the vigorous silhouette which a thousand photographs have already popularised throughout the world. It-was[9] Ibáñez.

1 de paso para.	2 sentir unos deseos.	3 pluma-pincel.
4 colegas de la pluma.	5 al atardecer.	6 vaivén.
7 *Los Argonautas*.	8 tener un gesto.	9 hé aquí.

42

Whilst amendments[1] to the tobacco tax were being discussed, the muffled and rapid noise of rain sounded on the sky-light. Here, I thought, is a valuable ally pronouncing itself in favour of the Government. Who does not know of the political importance of rain in these times? Previously it was the country which counted on[2] it as a decisive factor. Now, it is the town as well. It is not only agriculture, but industry, commerce, even public health, even the simple tasks of the home which are intimately bound up with this phenomenon. We-will-even-go-as-far-as-to-say[3] that it is in the country that the rain is of less importance. Farmers have determined with praiseworthy good sense that they cannot submit indefinitely to the caprice of the clouds, and they are[4] defending themselves with their canals and reservoirs. Whereas in the town..., in the town the streets are dirty, the culverts dry...the people are sick...and the municipal and sanitary authorities murmur: 'You-see,-there-is-no-rain![5]'...In the town the electric supply runs out; private people grumble..., the officials explain with regret: 'You-see,-there-is-no-rain![5]'

| 1 enmiendas. | 2 con. | 3 aun estamos por decir. |
| 4 ir. | 5 ¡como no llueve! | |

43

'Throughout Spain there is a fervent desire for work and prosperity. From every direction flows a strong sweeping[1] current which demands energetic and decided action on the part of the Government. My journeys are instructive, because in them I catch that atmosphere, so different from what we breathe here, in this confined circle. I believe, and I say it with sincerity, that this longing on the part of the country will have more strength than the political obstacles which stand-in-its-way[2], and that it will prevail over them. I, for my part, will not give way, as I never have given way, if it-is-a-question[3] of doing good for my country. I have spoken in Malaga, in Seville and in Cordoba; on Saturday I shall go to Valladolid where the railway-men[4] expect me; the following week I shall visit the irrigations of Upper[5] Aragon. I have faith in the patriotism of my countrymen; I have hopes that those who can help me will convince themselves that no other interest than that of my country moves me, and above all I have the determination not to retreat before difficulties, whatever they may be.'

| 1 arrolladora. | 2 cerrarle el paso. | 3 tratarse. |
| 4 ferroviarios. | 5 alto. | |

44

Catholic Spain, once more giving proofs of her religious feelings, has solemnised this year the greatest festival of the Church, which in *Corpus Christi* symbolises the institution of the Holy-Eucharist[1]. This festival is an-old-established-one[2] in the towns of Spain and is still invested with all its splendour by the towns of Granada, Murcia and Toledo, where are held magnificent processions and festivities, which recall to mind those which in the sixteenth century gave opportunities to some of our greatest geniuses—Lope de Vega, Tirso de Molina and Calderon—to write their celebrated *autos sacramentales*, to the delight of the people, who recognised in these works the most genuine expression of Spanish dramatic art. This year in Madrid the religious ceremonies had to be confined to the parish churches owing to the rainy weather. In Granada however the procession was[3] a superb spectacle.

1 Sagrada Eucaristia. 2 de tradicional abolengo. 3 resultar.

45

As was to be supposed, the English naval plans for the reorganisation of their fleet are beginning to take-shape[1]. It is fair to recognise that the British proposal to reinforce their navy does not imply the maintenance of that previous superiority, which consisted in possessing a fleet equal, at least, to that which any other two strong naval powers could bring together. At the moment English ambitions are confined to supporting a squadron which is[2] not inferior to any other, or more precisely, to construct the necessary number of vessels so that the British Fleet should not have, in the short period of three years, less strength than that of North America. Therefore, the determined attitude of the United States Government to get ready at-all-costs[3] a large navy has had the effect of diminishing the relative power of the English Navy. Within a short time, and theoretically dating from to-day, the English naval supremacy will be reduced to sharing with the United States the maritime domination of the world.

1 definirse. 2 *subjunctive*. 3 a todo trance.

46

Augusta Victoria, Queen of Prussia and Empress of Germany, was one of the sovereigns most worthy of esteem in modern Europe. Her name certainly will not figure amongst those of queens and empresses who took part in the politics of their respective nations, with greater or less success; she always lived apart from political struggles both[1] internal and[1] external, and if she had any effect on them, it was only that which was made inevitable by her position of intimacy. William II found, then, in Augusta Victoria a model wife, and his sons an exemplary mother. The singular exaltation of her position never perturbed her, and on the royal imperial throne she retained the kindly and modest behaviour of her home. The war surprised her (at a time when she was) happy in her home and beloved by the people; but death carried[2] her off[2] when she was dethroned and exiled, her tears scarcely dry after the suicide of one of her sons, the first whom she had seen die. In her bereavement she exhibited[3] great fortitude of mind, and rancour found no place in her heart. Of a profoundly Christian spirit, she gave to the women of her country and of the world a lofty example of simplicity in royalty and self-abnegation in misfortune.

1 así...como. 2 llevarse. 3 manifestar.

(N.B. *In the following four pieces the second person of the familiar form must be used.*)

47

And Elijah came near unto all the people, and said, How long halt[1] ye between two opinions? If the Lord be God, follow him: but if Baal[2], then follow him. And the people answered him not a word. Then said Elijah unto the people,

I, even I only, am left a prophet of the Lord; but Baal's prophets are four hundred and fifty men. Let them therefore give us two bullocks; and let them choose one bullock for themselves, and cut it in pieces, and lay it on the wood, and put no fire under: and I will dress[3] the other bullock, and lay it on the wood, and put no fire under. And call ye on the name of your god, and I will call on the name of the Lord: and the God that answereth by fire, let him be God. And all the people answered and said, It is well spoken. And Elijah said unto the prophets of Baal, Choose you one bullock for yourselves, and dress it first; for ye are many; and call on the name of your god, but put no fire under. And they took the bullock which was given them, and they dressed it, and called on the name of Baal from morning even unto noon, saying, O Baal, hear us. But there was no voice, nor any-that[4] answered. And they leapt about the altar which was made. And it came to pass at noon, that Elijah mocked them, and said, Cry aloud: for he is a god; either he is musing, or he is pursuing, or he is in a journey, or per-adventure he sleepeth, and must be awaked. And they cried aloud, and cut[5] themselves after[6] their manner with knives and lances[7], till the blood gushed-out[8] upon them. And it was so, when midday was past, that they prophesied until the time of the offering of the evening oblation[9]; but there was neither voice, nor any-to[4] answer, nor any that regarded.

1 cojear.	2 Bahal.	3 aparejar.
4 quien *with subjunctive*.	5 sajarse.	6 conforme a.
7 lanceta.	8 derramar.	9 sacrificio.

48

Strengthen ye the weak hands, and confirm the feeble knees. Say to them that are of a fearful heart[1], Be strong, fear not: behold[2], your God will come with vengeance,

with the recompence of God; he will come and save you.
Then the eyes of the blind shall be opened, and the ears of
the deaf shall be unstopped[3]. Then shall the lame man leap
as an hart, and the tongue of the dumb shall sing: for in
the wilderness shall waters break out, and streams in the
desert. And the glowing sand shall become a pool, and the
thirsty ground springs of water: in the habitation of jackals,
where they lay, shall be grass with reeds and rushes. And
an high way[4] shall be there, and a way, and it shall be called
The way of holiness; the unclean[5] shall not pass over it; but
it shall be for those: the wayfaring men, yea fools[6], shall
not err therein. No lion shall be there, nor shall any ravenous
beast go up thereon, they shall not be found there; but the
redeemed shall walk there: and the ransomed of the Lord
shall return, and come with singing unto Zion; and ever-
lasting joy shall be upon their heads: they shall obtain
gladness and joy, and sorrow and sighing[7] shall flee away.

1 los medrosos de corazon.   2 he aquí.   3 abrirse.   4 calzada.
5 inmundos.   6 insensatos. 7 gemido.

49

And when he was come forth upon the land, there met
him a certain man out of the city, who had devils[1]; and for
a long time he had worn no clothes, and abode not in any
house, but in the tombs. And when he saw Jesus, he cried
out, and fell down[2] before him, and with a loud voice said,
What have I to do with[3] thee, Jesus, thou Son of the Most
High God? I beseech thee, torment me not. And Jesus asked
him, What is thy name? And he said, Legion; for many
devils were entered into him. And they intreated him that
he would not command them to depart into the abyss[4]. Now
there was there a herd of many swine feeding[5] on the

mountain: and they intreated him that he would give them leave[6] to enter into them. And he gave them leave. And the devils came out from the man, and entered into the swine: and the herd rushed down the steep place[7] into the lake, and were choked. And all the people of the country of the Gerasenes round about[8] asked him to depart from them; for they were holden with great fear: and he entered into a boat, and returned.

1 demonios.   2 prostrarse.   3 ver con.   4 abismo.
5 pacer.   6 dejar.   7 despeñadero.   8 al derredor.

50

Rejoice alway[1]; pray without ceasing; in everything give thanks: for this is the will of God in Christ Jesus to youward[2]. Quench[3] not the Spirit; despise not prophesyings; prove all things; hold fast[4] that which is good; abstain[5] from every form of evil. And the God of peace himself sanctify you wholly[6]; and may your spirit and soul and body be preserved entire, without blame at the coming of our Lord Jesus Christ. Faithful is he that calleth you, who will also do it. Brethren, pray for us. Salute all the brethren with a holy kiss. I adjure you by the Lord that this epistle be read unto all the brethren. The grace of our Lord Jesus Christ be with you.

1 siempre.   2 acerca de.   3 apagar.   4 retener.
5 apartarse.   6 cabalmente.

APPENDIX

WORDS AND MEANINGS

§ 79. The following lists may be found useful. They contain 1. nouns, 2. adjectives, 3. verbs, whose meanings are easily confused owing to:

(a) resemblance with English words;

(b) resemblance with other Spanish words;

(c) separate meanings of the same words[1].

§ 80. 1. *Nouns.*

(a)	*Spanish*	*English*	*English*	*Spanish*
	éxito	success	exit	salida
	desmayo	faint	dismay	consternación (desmayo)
	desgracia	misfortune	disgrace	ignominia
	lectura	reading	lecture	conferencia
	bala	bullet	ball, dance	baile
	disgusto	displeasure	disgust	repugnancia (disgusto)
	ropa	clothes	rope	cuerda
	casualidad	chance	casualty	baja
	letra	letter of alphabet	letter	carta
	luto	mourning	lute	laúd
	plaza	square	place	sitio, lugar
	aviso	warning	advice	consejo
	campo	field	camp	campamento
	noticias	news	notice	aviso
	tabla	plank	table	mesa
	sopa	soup	soap	jabón
	bigote	moustache	bigot	fanático
	temple	temper	temple	templo
	capa	cloak	cape (geog.)	cabo

1 In many cases Latin derivations explain apparent discrepancies.

(b)

Spanish	English
data. dato. datil	date. information. date (fruit)
vela. veló	candle, sail. veil
amo. amigo	master. friend
hombre. hombro	man. shoulder
una. uña	one. finger-nail
puerta. puerto	door. harbour
rata. rato. ratón	rat. period of time. mouse
plaza. plazo	square. period of time
leche. lecho	milk. couch
cuadra. cuadro	stall. picture
aguja. agujero	needle. hole
dicha. dicho	happiness. said (pp. decir)
tormenta. tormento	storm. torment

(c)

matrimonio	marriage. married couple
silla	chair. saddle
natural	natural (adj.). native
motivo	motive. occasion, time, reason, etc.[1]
puro	pure (adj.). cigar
fuente	fountain. dish of food
cabo	cape (geog.). corporal
esposas	wives. handcuffs
manzana	apple. block of houses

2. *Adjectives.*

(a)

Spanish	English	English	Spanish
blando	soft	bland	suave
largo	long	large	grande
listo	ready	list (noun)	lista

(b)

Spanish	English
cuerdo. cuerda	clever. rope
reciente. recio	recent. strong

1 *con motivo de* is a common expression having many meanings.

Spanish	English
(c) distinto	different. distinct
gracioso	gracious. witty
precioso	precious. pretty. witty
real	royal. real (real, 2½d.)

3. Verbs.

(a) Spanish	English	English	Spanish
quitar	take away	quit, leave	salir
suceder	happen	succeed	lograr, conseguir
contestar	answer	contest	contender
convenir	suit	convene	convocar
gritar	shout	greet	saludar
sacar	draw out	sack	saquear

(b) Spanish	English
carecer. encarecer	lack. praise highly
alentar. alimentar	encourage. feed
amenazar. amanecer	threaten. dawn
ahogar. ahorcar. ahorrar	stifle, drown. hang. save money
asar. asear	roast. adorn (personal)
atrever. atravesar	dare. cross
pasar. pasear	pass. walk
dividir. divisar	divide. catch sight of
crear. criar	create. bring up
entrar. enterar. enterrar	enter. inform. bury
remedar. remediar	imitate. remedy
rodear. rodar	surround. wheel, roll
sonar. soñar	sound. dream
quedar. quemar. quejar	remain. burn. complain
abrasar. abrazar	burn. embrace
acudir. sacudir	hasten. shake
jugar. juzgar.	play. judge
arrastrar. arrostrar	drag. face
negar. anegar	deny. drown
rezar. rizar. rozar	pray. curl. graze

Spanish	English
(c) admirar	admire. astonish
ignorar	ignore. not to know
apurar-se	drain. worry
empeñar-se	pledge. desire strongly
obligar	oblige. compel
acertar	hit a mark. be right
referir	refer. relate
despedir-se	dismiss. say good-bye
pegar	stick. hit
esperar	hope. wait for
pesar	weigh. grieve

The above lists do not claim to be complete and spaces have been left in order that words may be added.

For EU product safety concerns, contact us at Calle de José Abascal, 56–1°,
28003 Madrid, Spain or eugpsr@cambridge.org.

www.ingramcontent.com/pod-product-compliance
Ingram Content Group UK Ltd.
Pitfield, Milton Keynes, MK11 3LW, UK
UKHW012333130625
459647UK00009B/265